A GUIDE TO READING SHAKESPEARE'S *HAMLET*

A GUIDE TO READING SHAKESPEARE'S *HAMLET*

MARIA FRANZISKA FAHEY

Maria Franziska Fahey is the author of *Metaphor and Shakespearean Drama: Unchaste Signification*, which was shortlisted for the 2012 Shakespeare's Globe Book Award. She is a member of the faculty at Friends Seminary, where she has taught English for more than twenty-five years.

Copyright © 2013 by Maria Franziska Fahey

All rights reserved.

Except for the use of brief quotations in a book review, no part of this book may be reproduced in any form by any electronic or mechanical means without the express written permission of the author.

First Printing, 2013
Second Printing, 2014, contains corrections and minor revisions of the text.
Third Printing, 2022, contains corrections and minor revisions of the text.

ISBN-13: 978-0615872445
ISBN-10: 0615872441

Accabonac Press
61 Jane Street, Suite 17C, New York, NY 10014

Cover illustration and design by Lauren Simkin Berke

CONTENTS

Preface vii
    On the Pleasures & Challenges of Reading Shakespeare's Dramatic Language vii
    Using This Guide viii
    Hearing & Seeing Performances ix

Questions to Consider as You Read *Hamlet* 1
    Larger Questions 1
    Patterns of Figurative Language 2
    Act 1, Scene 1 3
    Act 1, Scene 2 9
    Act 1, Scene 3 18
    Act 1, Scene 4 23
    Act 1, Scene 5 25
    Act 2, Scene 1 33
    Act 2, Scene 2 36
    Act 3, Scene 1 48
    Act 3, Scene 2 55
    Act 3, Scene 3 61
    Act 3, Scene 4 64
    Act 4, Scene 1 71
    Act 4, Scene 2 72
    Act 4, Scene 3 73
    Act 4, Scene 4 74
    Act 4, Scene 5 77
    Act 4, Scene 6 82
    Act 4, Scene 7 83
    Act 5, Scene 1 84
    Act 5, Scene 2 88

Appendices 93
    1. Listening for Meter—An Introduction 93
    2. Reading Figurative Language—An Introduction to Metaphor, Simile, Metonymy, &
    Synecdoche 97
    3. On How an Edition of *Hamlet* Is Made 104

Acknowledgments 107

PREFACE

On the Pleasures & Challenges of Reading Shakespeare's Dramatic Language

Reading Shakespeare's plays can be immensely pleasurable, but doing so is no easy task. Whereas we now get a great deal of our information through visual images, including photographs and film, in Shakespeare's day most information came through spoken language. Part of the fun, and also the challenge, of reading a Shakespeare play is having to transform language into visual images for ourselves.

Indeed, Shakespeare was aware of the demands he was making of his audiences. In the Prologue to his play *The Life of Henry the Fifth*, the Chorus admits that it cannot bring King Henry himself or "the vasty fields of France" into the theater and so asks the members of the audience to let the play work on their "imaginary forces" (*Henry V* Pro. 12, 18). The Chorus goes on to suggest, "Think, when we talk of horses, that you see them, / Printing their proud hoofs i'th' receiving earth" (Pro. 26-7).

A Shakespeare play is largely "talk"—a series of conversations among a cast of characters. However, the talk of a Shakespeare play is often more difficult to understand than ordinary speech because it has been crafted to bring a whole world before our eyes. The series of questions in this guide is designed to help you listen carefully, scene-by-scene, to what the characters say so that you can use your "imaginary forces" to see the world of *Hamlet* for yourself. As you read the play's language and begin to envision its world, it will be helpful to remain aware of how the language spoken by characters in the play is different from that of ordinary speech. Here are a few of these differences:

Vocabulary. Written over 400 years ago, the plays are known for their unusually large vocabularies, including many words that were, at the time, new to the English language—some probably invented by Shakespeare himself. Almost all readers find the rich vocabulary of a Shakespeare play challenging to understand even as they come to enjoy the subtle and abundant connotations of the words Shakespeare chose. Furthermore, twenty-first century readers will find that the meanings of some words have changed since Shakespeare's day and that other words, rarely spoken now, have become obsolete. For instance, the word *sometime* in King Claudius's reference to Queen Gertrude as "our sometime sister, now our queen" (*Hamlet* 1.2.8) means *former*—not *occasional* as it might now. Be sure to consult the notes in your copy of the play and to keep a good dictionary at hand, one that provides older meanings of words. (Check your library's print or online version of *The Oxford English Dictionary*—the *OED*—which is the most comprehensive English dictionary.)

But don't feel obligated to look up every word when first reading a play. You can understand a great deal about unfamiliar words from their context. For instance, Hamlet tells Ophelia, "We are arrant knaves, all: believe none of us" (*Hamlet* 3.1.128). You might not know what a *knave* is or what *arrant* means. But you can figure out that if Hamlet tells Ophelia to "believe none of us" after announcing that they are all "arrant knaves," then an *arrant knave* must be an untrustworthy man. (The *Oxford English Dictionary* indicates that "arrant" can mean "notorious" or "downright" and that a "knave" is "an unprincipled man.")

Poetic Language. The conversations in a Shakespeare play are no ordinary conversations: they were crafted by a poet-playwright who used sound, rhythm, and imagery to convey his meanings. Consider King Claudius's remark that ends the scene in which he tries, unsuccessfully, to pray:

> My words fly up, my thoughts remain below:
> Words without thoughts never to heaven go.   (*Hamlet* 3.3.97-8)

In ordinary speech, someone would likely say, "Words without thoughts *never go to heaven*." But Shakespeare's word order allows the lines to rhyme—"below" with "go"—which adds a finality to Claudius's conclusion and to the scene. Sometimes Shakespeare's language demands a bit of extra thinking as you listen for the meanings of a character's words along with the meanings added by sound, rhythm, and imagery. *(See appendices 1 and 2 for an introduction to meter and figurative language.)*

⚜ ***Descriptions that Provide Context.*** Although Shakespeare's theater included costumes and some props, it did not include sets or lighting. (The use of electricity was centuries away, and plays were performed at The Globe, an open-air theater, in the mid-afternoon.) Audiences would have to glean important context from the characters' speeches. For instance, in *Hamlet*'s first scene, we learn that the sun is rising when a character poetically describes the early morning as if it were a person wearing a reddish-brown cloak walking over the dew on a hill in the east:

> But, look, the morn, in russet mantle clad,
> Walks o'er the dew of yon high eastward hill. (*Hamlet* 1.1.166-7)

Nowadays such a transition from night to morning could be shown to a theater audience with lighting design, and a painted set could show the hill. Thus, contemporary playwrights usually don't write such descriptions into characters' speeches, and contemporary audiences don't have to decipher and picture them.

⚜ ***Implied Action.*** Unlike stories or novels, most plays don't have a narrator who tells us what characters are doing as they speak to each other. Playwrights can indicate specific actions with stage directions, but Shakespeare's plays have relatively few. Instead, the dialogue itself gives clues about characters' actions. Consider this exchange about the Ghost that has appeared to Prince Hamlet and his friends:

> *Hamlet*   It waves me still. Go on; I'll follow thee.
> *Marcellus* You shall not go my lord.
> *Hamlet*   Hold off your hands.
> *Horatio*   Be ruled.   (*Hamlet* 1.4.78-80)

Hamlet's first line lets us see the Ghost waving to Hamlet, indicating that it wants Hamlet to follow. Hamlet's second line, "Hold off your hands," lets us see Marcellus and Horatio physically holding Hamlet, attempting to stop him from following the Ghost. Imagining the world of a Shakespeare play depends, in part, on listening for clues to characters' actions. (Try staging a scene with some friends: doing so will help you become attentive to such clues.)

Learning to see the world of a Shakespeare play by reading or hearing its language takes some work and some patience. However, paying close attention to the play's language will give you access to the most interesting, complicated, and surprising aspects of the plays. As the Prologue to *The Life of Henry the Fifth* shows, Shakespeare invited and relied on his audiences to envision the worlds of his plays, and Shakespeare gave us incomparable language from which to do so. There are always many ways to imagine a phrase, line, or scene, but it's important to start with accurate observations of the play's language.

Using This Guide

The series of questions for each scene will help you to observe the sometimes complex and dense language accurately and to puzzle through the characters' conversations. Before trying to answer the questions for a particular scene, read through the entire scene aloud. Or, better yet, gather some friends, take parts, and read the scene aloud together. Don't be shy: you might mispronounce a word or need to read some lines slowly, but you will have a much better chance of understanding the lines when you read them aloud—and you likely will have more fun. Then, read through the scene again slowly, answering the questions as you go. If you don't fully understand a question, quote the phrase or line that you suspect contains the clues for its answer. Once you reach the scene's end, return to those questions to see if you have been able to figure out anything further.

Some of the questions use terms and refer to methods with which you may not be familiar: they may ask you to observe and analyze "meter" or "figurative language," especially "metaphor." Don't worry if you are not familiar with these terms or if you never have "scanned a line of verse" or "sorted a metaphor's tenor and vehicle": you will find the necessary background information and sample analyses in the appendices. Appendix 1, "Listening for Meter," explains how to identify the basic rhythms of Shakespeare's poetry; appendix 2, "Reading Figurative Language," explains how to identify and analyze figures of speech; and appendix 3, "On How an Edition of *Hamlet* Is Made," explains how the copy of *Hamlet* you are reading is derived from the earliest texts of the play and lets you know what kinds of additions and changes an editor may have made in preparing the play for publication. You may find it helpful to read through these appendices before you begin to answer the questions. Or you may consult them when you arrive at a question that requires your knowledge of the information they provide. All of the information in the appendices aims to help you to understand and envision the play for yourself.

Quotations in this guide are taken from the edition of *Hamlet* edited by Burton Raffel and published by Yale University Press in 2003. Following standard scholarly practice, quotations are followed by a citation that indicates the act, scene, and lines from which a passage is quoted. So, for instance, "(3.1.6-7)" refers to act 3, scene 1, lines 6-7. If you are reading a different edition of the play, your line numbers may be slightly different. *(See appendix 3, "On How an Edition of Hamlet Is Made," for an explanation of how the differences in editions come about.)*

Hearing & Seeing Performances

If, after trying to read aloud by yourself and with friends, you continue to have trouble getting the gist of what the characters are saying to each other, try to locate a good audio recording of the play, one that has been recorded by a cast of experienced Shakespearean actors. (Many libraries have such recordings available.) Read along as you listen to the audio recording of the scene you are working on. Hearing trained actors deliver the characters' lines will likely help you understand much of what the characters are saying. Keep in mind that the way an actor speaks a line depends on that actor's interpretation of it and that you might have another interpretation.

After reading the play, you might enjoy seeing a performance of it. Check to see if there is a live performance at a nearby theater or borrow a film of the play from your library. If you wait to see a performance until after reading the play, you will be able to compare the way you have imagined the play-world to the way a particular director has. If you see the performance before you've read the play, be aware, as you read, that the particular director's vision of the play is not the only possibility: one good way to do so is to see two, or more, performances or films.

There are many books and websites that publish summaries and analyses of Shakespeare's plays. Be wary. Don't accept another reader's vision of the play too easily: your own careful reading and imagining might lead you to a far more interesting one!

QUESTIONS TO CONSIDER AS YOU READ *HAMLET*

Larger Questions

As you answer the questions for each scene, you often will be prompted to think about the topics listed below. If you are particularly interested in one of these topics, you might find it helpful to keep track of what various characters say about it by marking relevant passages in your text or by keeping a list of relevant passages in a notebook. When you have finished reading the play, you then will be ready to consider the collection of passages you have gathered and ask yourself what the play as a whole might be suggesting about the topic. This kind of work is one way to prepare to write an essay about *Hamlet*.

1. **Seeming & Being**. What do characters say about seeming? About being? What does the play as a whole suggest about the relationship between seeming and being?

2. **Acting, Playing, Showing, & Seeming**. What is the role of acting within *Hamlet*? How do the plays and the speeches performed by professional actors function? Aside from these professional actors, who else in *Hamlet* acts? For what purpose? With what consequences?

3. **Nature**. How and when do characters talk about nature? What do characters assert is *natural*? What do they assert is *unnatural*?

4. **Beasts, Humans, & Gods**. What do characters say makes people like beasts? What makes them like gods? What do these comparisons imply it means to be human?

5. **Sons & Daughters, Mothers & Fathers, Sisters & Brothers**. What responsibilities, privileges, and obligations do characters assert, or imply, come with one's position in a family?

6. **Kingship**. What do various characters say about the nature of kingship? About the sources of a king's authority? About the responsibilities of a king? About the duties of a subject? What light does the play as a whole cast on these various assertions about kingship?

7. **Blood & Judgment**. What do characters say about the relationship between "blood" or passion and "judgment" or reason? What do they say is the influence of each on human action or inaction? How do characters' assertions about the effects of "conscience" fit in?

8. **Belief & Faith, Sense & Reason**. On what basis do characters claim to know what they know? What does the play as a whole suggest about the relationship between faith and reason?

9. **Madness**. What actions—and what kinds of speech—are judged as signs of lunacy, madness, distraction, or distemper? What does Hamlet do after telling his friends he will "put an antic disposition on" (1.5.172)? What do characters assert are the causes of madness?

10. **Remembering & Forgetting**. What do characters say about remembering and forgetting? How are remembering and forgetting important? How are they dangerous? With what figures of speech do characters describe memory?

11. **Honor**. What do characters say about honor? What acts are considered honorable? What does the play *Hamlet* suggest about these notions of honor?

12. **Customs, Rites, & Habits**. What are characters' attitudes toward customs and rites? What, in particular, are their attitudes toward funeral rites? When are customs followed and rites performed? When are they broken? What does the play overall seem to suggest about the consequences of following customs? Of breaking them?

13. **Revenge & Forgiveness**. What prompts revenge? What motivates forgiveness? What do characters say about revenge? What does the play *Hamlet* overall show about revenge and forgiveness?

14. **Grief, Mourning, & Pity**. What do characters say about grief and mourning? About pity? What emerges about the relationship between reason and mourning?

15. **Fate, Fortune, Providence, & Destiny**. What do characters say about destiny? When do they invoke the gods or God?

Patterns of Figurative Language

Questions for each scene also will prompt you to notice and analyze figurative language. *(See appendix 1 for an introduction to figurative language.)* Sometimes one instance of figurative language echoes figurative language from other scenes in the play. These patterns of figurative language are an important part of how the play is structured and delivers its meanings. You might find it helpful to keep track of repeating figures by marking instances of them in your text or by keeping a list in a notebook. When you have finished reading the play, you then will be ready to ask yourself what the pattern suggests or means. In *Hamlet*, be on the lookout for figures of:

1. Ears
2. Speech, Words, Vows, Slander, & Flattery
3. Rot, Corruption, Smells, Rankness, Compost, & Maggots
4. Diseases & Cures
5. Poison
6. Makeup, Painting, & Color
7. Suits, Cloaks, Trappings, Garb, Frocks, Livery, & Habits
8. Covering, Clothing, & Cloaking
9. Uncovering, Unfolding, & Disclosing
10. Whores, Bawds, Strumpets, & Harlots
11. Beasts
12. Mirrors & Glasses
13. Pictures, Likenesses, & Paintings
14. Things & Nothing

ACT 1, SCENE 1

1. Notice that the play opens with a question. If Francisco is on guard and Barnardo has come to relieve him, how is Barnardo's question surprising?

2. Indeed, Francisco demands, instead, that the approaching Barnardo "Stand and unfold" himself (1.1.2). How does Barnardo do so?

3. What does Francisco add to his observation that it is "bitter cold" (1.1.8)?

4. What is Horatio's attitude toward the report on the apparition?

    a. Jot down a few of Marcellus and Horatio's key phrases.

    b. Considering what Horatio has said about the apparition, why would he join the watch? Give two possibilities.

5. Analyze Barnardo's metaphor: "And let us once again assail your ears, / That are so fortified against our story / What we have two nights seen" (1.1.31-3). *(For an explanation of the terms and method of analysis, see pages 97-103 of appendix 1, "Reading Figurative Language.")*

vehicle	:	tenor
assail	:	_____
_____	:	ears
fortified	:	_____
_____	:	story

   What does Barnardo's metaphor imply about speech? About listening?

6. Count the number of times that Marcellus, Barnardo, and Horatio refer to the apparition as "it"—just in the first six lines of their remarks (1.1.40-5). Then, count the number of times they use the word "like." What do their remarks—and their specific language—suggest about their understanding of the apparition?

7. What exactly does Horatio ask the Ghost (1.1.46-9)?

8. When Marcellus points out, "Look where it comes again," Barnardo observes, "In the same figure like the King that's dead" (1.1.40-1). A bit later when Marcellus asks Horatio, "Is it not like the king" (1.1.58), Horatio responds, "As thou art to thyself" (1.1.59). What exactly have they concluded about the relationship between the apparition and the dead king?

9. Horatio goes on to describe "its" appearance: what impression does this description leave about what the former king was "like"?

10. What does Horatio conclude that the apparition "bodes" (1.1.67-9)? (*Bodes* means announce, foretell [*OED* 3]).

11. Marcellus asks a long question: he wants to know the reason for the war preparations (1.1.70-9). What do we learn about the current state of Denmark from the descriptions of Denmark in his question?

12. What do we learn from Horatio's answer about the conflict between "our last king" Hamlet and "Fortinbras of Norway" (1.1.79-95)? What was the conflict's outcome?

13. What do we learn about young Fortinbras's current activities (1.1.95-104)?

14. What does Barnardo say now about "this portentous figure" (1.1.109)? (*Portentous* means ominous, threatening [*OED* 1]).

15. EXTRA OPPORTUNITY.

    a. If you were making a film of Horatio's story about Rome (1.1.113-20), what would it include?

    b. Horatio ends his story by comparing that moment in Rome to the present moment in Denmark:

    > And even the like precurse of fierce events,
    > As harbingers preceding still the fates
    > And prologue to the omen coming on,
    > Have heaven and earth together demonstrated
    > Unto our climatures and countrymen (1.1.121-5).

    How did Julius Caesar "fall"? What is the effect of Horatio's comparison of the portentous events in Rome before Julius fell to the portentous events in Denmark?

16. When the apparition reappears, about what does Horatio want it to speak (1.1.128-39)?

17. Marcellus asks, "Shall I strike at it with my partisan" (1.1.140)? Do you think striking the ghost would be effective? What does Marcellus's question suggest about his experience of the Ghost?

18. Horatio, Barnardo, and Marcellus's comments about how the Ghost reacts to the cock crowing contain clues about how to perform the role of the Ghost (1.1.147-57). List three key phrases or lines that would be important to consider if you were playing the Ghost.

19. EXTRA OPPORTUNITY. Marcellus tells a story about the season of "our Saviour's birth" (1.1.158-64).

    a. What has Marcellus heard about the night of Jesus's birth?

    b. What does this story add to the appearance of the apparition?

20. What is Horatio's reason for suggesting that they go tell "young Hamlet" about the spirit (1.1.169-71)?

21. Review the scene: What have Marcellus, Barnardo, and Horatio concluded about the Ghost? About what are they unsure? Derive your answers from specific lines and phrases.

ACT 1, SCENE 2

As you read King Claudius's opening speech, note that he uses the so-called "royal we": he refers to himself as king with plural pronouns, such as, "we," "us," "our," and "ourself."

1. Reread Claudius's first long sentence (1.2.1-7).

    a. What is the topic of the opening subordinate clause ("Though yet of Hamlet . . . brow of woe,")?

    b. What is the topic of the closing independent clause? (Yet, so far . . . ourselves.")?

    c. On which clause does the sentence place more weight?

2. Reread Claudius's second sentence (1.2.8-14). List six paradoxes that lead to Claudius's announcement of his marriage.

3. What might motivate King Claudius to articulate publicly the contradictions and paradoxes of this moment in Denmark and of his marriage? What does this speech reveal about the kind of statesman Claudius is?

4. What plan does Claudius announce for dealing with young Fortinbras? How are Cornelius and Voltemand involved (1.2.17-39)?

5. What more do we learn about the kingship and royal family in Norway (1.2.28-38)? (Note that "Norway" (1.2.28) can refer to the King of Norway as well as the country of Norway.) Parallels to the situation in Denmark? Differences?

6. How does Claudius respond to Laertes's request? How does Claudius treat Laertes? Jot down two or three key phrases.

7. In Shakespeare's day, *cousin* had the more general meaning of "a relative" and "very frequently applied to a nephew or niece" (*OED* 1a *Obs.*). In what way does Claudius's greeting, "But now, my cousin Hamlet, and my son" warrant Hamlet's response, "A little more than kin" (1.2.64-5)?

8. Each of Hamlet's first two lines in the play contains a pun. Consider these puns and explain two or more meanings each of Hamlet's lines conveys.

    (A *pun* is the use of a word in a statement that simultaneously suggests two or more meanings of the word and, thus, two or more ways to understand the statement. A speaker can make a pun on a word that has more than one meaning or on a word that sounds like another word.)

    a. "A little more than kin, and less than <u>kind</u>." (1.2.65) (Understood as a noun, *kind* can mean, "a natural quality" [*OED* 6] or "offspring or descendents" [*OED* 11b]. As an adjective, *kind* can mean, "having a gentle, sympathetic, or benevolent nature" [*OED* 5a].)

    b. "Not so, my lord. I am too much i' the <u>sun</u>." (1.2.67) (*Sun* sounds like *son*.)

9. Although there is no stage direction in any of the early texts of *Hamlet*, the Yale edition marks Hamlet's first line, "A little more than kin, and less than kind," as "(*aside*)." (See pages 104-6 of appendix 3, "On How an Edition of Hamlet is Made," for an introduction to the early texts.)

    a. What would be the effect of Hamlet's saying this line as an aside? What would be the effect of Hamlet's saying it directly to Claudius?

    b. If you were directing *Hamlet*, how would you direct the actor playing Hamlet to deliver the line? Write your own stage direction.

10. What might motivate Gertrude to interject? Propose two tones with which she might say, "Good Hamlet, cast thy nighted color off . . . " (1.2.68-73).

11. Which image does Gertrude pick up when she advises Hamlet, "cast thy nighted color off" (1.2.68)? What might Gertrude's comment suggest about how Hamlet is behaving? About what he is wearing?

12. Reread Hamlet's first long speech carefully; it begins, "Seems, madam! nay, it is: I know not 'seems'" (1.2.76-86).

    a. "'Tis not alone . . . / That can denote me truly" (1.2.77). What are the things that Hamlet claims cannot denote him truly? List them.

    b. Why, according to Hamlet, can these things not denote him truly? Quote and explain the line that contains the answer.

    c. If you were playing Hamlet, to what could you gesture as you said, "*These* but the trappings and the suits of woe" (1.2.85, emphasis mine)?

    d. Considering its context and the speech that follows, explain what Hamlet might mean when he claims, "I know not 'seems'" (1.2.76).

13. Reread Claudius's response to Hamlet: "'Tis sweet and commendable in your nature, Hamlet . . . Our chiefest courtier, cousin, and our son." (1.2.87-117).

   a. With what tone might Claudius say "sweet and commendable" (1.2.87)? Give two possibilities.

   b. Of what does Claudius accuse Hamlet?

   c. What lesson does Claudius teach about appropriate mourning for the dead?

   d. EXTRA OPPORTUNITY. Who, according to the Book of Genesis, was "the first corse" (1.2.105)? How did the man who was the first corpse die? What does Claudius's reference add to this scene?

   e. What does Claudius pronounce when he says, "think of us / As of a father, for let the world take note / You are most immediate to our throne" (1.2.107-9)?

   f. On what basis does Claudius deny Hamlet's request to go "back to school in Wittenberg" (1.2.113)?

g. EXTRA RESEARCH OPPORTUNITY. For what would Wittenberg have been famous in Shakespeare's day, as it is now?

h. Why might Claudius not want Hamlet to leave Denmark to go back to school? Why might Gertrude not want Hamlet to leave?

14. Reread Hamlet's first soliloquy: "O, that this too too solid flesh would melt . . . But break my heart, for I must hold my tongue" (1.2.129-58).

   a. For what does Hamlet wish ("O, that this . . . / Or that . . . .")?

   b. Hamlet asserts that the world is "an unweeded garden / That grows to seed: things rank and gross in nature / Possess it merely" (1.2.135-37). Analyze the metaphor:

   vehicle   :   tenor

   c. What does this particular metaphor tell us about Hamlet's sense of the world? Think carefully about the vehicle of the *unweeded garden*. (You might consider how it would be different for Hamlet to say the world is a *jungle*.)

d. For how long has Hamlet's father been dead?

e. Whom does Hamlet compare to the hyperion (a sun god)? To the satyr (a semi-divine creature, part human-part goat)?

   hyperion: _____

   satyr: _____

f. What does Hamlet remember about the way his father treated his mother?

g. What does Hamlet remember about the way his mother acted toward his father?

h. "Let me not think on't: frailty, thy name is woman" (1.2.146)? What is the "it" about which Hamlet tries to avoid thinking?

i. What, then, leads Hamlet to assert, "frailty, thy name is woman"? "Does Hamlet provide evidence about any woman other than Gertrude?

j. "[A] beast that wants discourse of reason / Would have mourned longer" (1.2.150-1). What does Hamlet imply about mourning? How does this idea compare to Claudius's remarks about mourning?

k. Why might Hamlet think he must "hold [his] tongue" (1.2.159)? Give two possibilities.

l. Review the speech. About what is Hamlet most upset? What do you notice about the way his mind is working here?

15. How does Prince Hamlet treat Horatio, Marcellus, and Bernardo? Quote one or two phrases from which you derive your answer.

16. With what tone might Hamlet remark, "The funeral baked meats / Did coldly furnish forth the marriage tables" (1.2.180-1)?

17. What might Horatio be thinking when he asks, "Where my Lord?" (1.2.185)? Write a stage direction for Horatio as he says this line.

18. Review 1.2.195-253 (starting "For God's love let me hear" and ending "Your loves, as mine to you. Farewell"). What is Hamlet's reaction to the news of the apparition? What do his questions show that he is concerned about or is trying to figure out? Quote two specific lines or phrases from which you derive your answers.

19. Reread Hamlet's speech that follows Horatio, Marcellus, and Barnardo's exit (1.2.255-8).

    a. What does Hamlet call the apparition now?

    b. If you were playing Hamlet, what "foul deed" might you have in mind?

ACT 1, SCENE 3

1. What imagery does Laertes use in advising Ophelia how to consider Hamlet's "favor" (1.3.5-9)? Quote key phrases.

2. Why, according to Laertes, is Hamlet's "will . . . not his own" (1.3.17)?

3. By what, according to Laertes, "must [Hamlet's] choice be circumscribed" (1.3.22)?

4. What does Laertes warn Ophelia might cause her loss of "honor" (1.3.29-32)? Note the imagery.

5. Do you think Laertes's warning makes sense?

6. What does Laertes mean when he asserts that "Virtue itself 'scapes not calumnious strokes" (1.3.38)? (*Calumnious* means "slanderous, defamatory" [*OED* 1].) Do you agree with Laertes about this?

7. Given what Laertes asserts about calumny, what is he implying that Ophelia should do?

8. EXTRA OPPORTUNITY. Reread Laertes's speech aloud and consider possibilities for his tone of voice and Ophelia's nonverbal reactions. Imagine that you are directing the scene, and write a stage direction or two for Laertes and Ophelia each, indicating at what lines you would insert the directions.

9. What does Ophelia say in response to her brother's lecture? With what tone might she say this? Give two possibilities.

10. What "few precepts" does Polonius want Laertes to remember when he is in France (1.3.58-81)? List a few:

11. In what light does the play *Hamlet* present the oft-quoted, "to thine own self be true" (1.3.78)? How does the advice compare to the other advice Polonius has given Laertes?

12. EXTRA OPPORTUNITY. If you were directing the scene, how would you instruct the actor playing Laertes to behave as his father gives this advice? What about Ophelia?

13. If you were Polonius, how would you feel when Ophelia tells Laertes that what he has said to her "is in [her] memory locked" (1.3.85)? Why might Ophelia say this?

14. What does Polonius assert about the time Ophelia has been spending with Hamlet?

15. How does Ophelia use the word *tender*? How does Polonius play with the word's meanings when he echoes it—four times—in his response (1.3.99-109)? Define the word's meaning in each context:

   a. He hath ... made many tenders / Of his affections to me. (1.3.99)

   b. Do you believe his tenders, as you call them? (1.3.103)

   c. Think ... / That you have ta'en these tenders for true pay / Which are not sterling. (1.3.106)

   d. Tender yourself more dearly; (1.3.107)

   e. Or ... you'll tender me a fool. (1.3.108-9)
   (Note: *Fool* could mean a "person without sense" or a "baby.")

16. With what metaphor does Polonius describe vows (1.3.115)? Quote the phrase.

17. Polonius describes Hamlet as being able to walk "with a larger tether" than Ophelia (1.3.125). Into what does this metaphor turn Hamlet and Ophelia?

18. Polonius uses another metaphor for vows. He says they are "brokers" (1.3.127). Referring to what he goes on to say, try to explain what he means.

19. How might Ophelia say, "I shall obey, my lord" in response to her father's command that she not talk with Hamlet (1.3.136)? Try saying the line in three different ways, expressing three different possible attitudes Ophelia has toward her father and toward Hamlet. Then, list three adjectives that describe those attitudes.

20. Review the scene. What do we learn about Polonius's relationship to his children in this scene? What is Polonius's attitude toward the world in which he and his children live? Toward men and women? What, in his advice to his daughter, does he unwittingly reveal about himself? You might think in particular about the lines: "I do know, / When the blood burns, how prodigal the soul / Lends the tongue vow" (1.3.115-17).

ACT 1, SCENE 4

1. Reread the first twelve lines of the scene and make a quick sketch of the scene. Where is Hamlet and what is he doing? Where is Claudius and what is he doing? How might Hamlet's location reflect how he feels about his place in Denmark?

2. Reread Hamlet's lengthy answer to Horatio's question about custom, which starts, "Ay marry, is't" (1.4.14-38):

   a. What does Hamlet mean when he says that Claudius's revelry is "a custom / More honored in the breach than the observance" (1.4.15-16)? What does Hamlet say about the Danes' reputation?

   b. Hamlet goes on to make a more general point about the human condition. What, according to Hamlet, happens to men "Carrying . . . the stamp of one defect" (1.4.31)? Quote and explain the lines from which you derive your answer.

   c. Paraphrase: "The dram of evil / Doth all of the noble substance often doubt, / To his own scandal" (1.4.36-8).

d. Do you agree with Hamlet about that the effects of "stamp of one defect" and "the dram of evil"? Why or why not?

e. EXTRA OPPORTUNITY. Notice that Horatio's announcement of the Ghost's arrival completes Hamlet's iambic pentameter line about the dram of evil (1.4.38):

> *Hamlet* To his own scandal.
> *Horatio*   Look, my lord, it comes!

What is the effect of the Ghost's arrival during this particular speech?

3. Upon seeing the Ghost, Hamlet says, "Angels and ministers of grace defend us!" (1.4.39). What does this appeal to the angels reveal about Hamlet's attitude toward the Ghost?

4. Although Hamlet is unsure whether the Ghost is a "spirit of health, or goblin damned" (1.4.40), what, nonetheless, does he decide to call it? What does he ask it?

5. What reasons does Horatio give for warning Hamlet not to follow the Ghost (1.4.69-78)?

6. Look for staging clues. For instance, what stage directions are implied by Hamlet's lines: "Unhand me, gentlemen. / By heaven, I'll make a ghost of him that lets me!" (1.4.84-5)? Write a stage direction for Hamlet and another for Horatio and Marcellus:

7. What does Marcellus conclude (1.4.90)? Fill in the blank: "Something is _____ in the state of Denmark."

ACT 1, SCENE 5

1. EXTRA RESEARCH OPPORTUNITY. The Ghost tells Hamlet that soon he must "render up" himself "to sulf'rous and tormenting flames" (1.5.3-4) and that during the day he is "confined to fast in fires, / Till the foul crimes done in [his] days of nature / Are burnt and purged away" (1.5.11-13). With what religious tradition is the purgatory the Ghost describes associated? With what religious tradition is Wittenberg, where Hamlet and Horatio were at school, associated? What is the official religion of England when *Hamlet* was written, namely, the late 1500s-early 1600s? What had it been before?

2. Note well the exchange below. What does it reveal about the Ghost's beliefs about revenge?

   Hamlet   Speak; I am bound to hear.
   Ghost   So art thou to revenge, when thou shalt hear.   (1.5.6-7)

3. The Ghost rejects Hamlet's pity: "Pity me not" (1.5.5). If the Ghost asserts that Hamlet is "bound" to revenge, what does the Ghost imply about pity and revenge?

4. Why, according to the Ghost, will he not tell Hamlet his harrowing story?

5. Explain the Ghost's assertion about murder: "Murder most foul, as in the best it is, / But this most foul, strange and unnatural" (1.5.27-8). What might be murder "in the best"? What makes this murder "most foul, strange and unnatural"?

6. What does the Ghost's assertion about murder imply about the Ghost's command that Hamlet revenge his father's murder? If you were Hamlet, how would you feel about what you were hearing from the Ghost?

7. Reread:

> 'Tis given out that, sleeping in my orchard,   35
> A serpent stung me. So the whole ear of Denmark
> Is by a forgèd process of my death
> Rankly abused. But know, thou noble youth,
> The serpent that did sting thy father's life
> Now wears his crown. (1.5.35-40)   40

    a. What story have people in Denmark heard about how King Hamlet died?

    b. What, according to the Ghost, really happened?

    c. In what two ways does the Ghost use the word *serpent*? How in line 36? How in line 39?

d. Explain to what the Ghost refers with the phrase, "the whole ear of Denmark" (1.5.36). What kind of figure of speech is "ear"—Metonymy, metaphor, or both? Explain your reasons. (For an explanation of *metonymy* and of the difference between *metaphor* and *metonymy*, see page 103 of appendix 2, "Reading Figurative Language.")

e. What is it, according to the Ghost, that has "[r]ankly abused" the "ear of Denmark"? Fill in the blanks and then explain in your own words.

So the whole ear of Denmark / Is by a _____ _____ of my death / Rankly abused.

8. How does Hamlet's response, "O my prophetic soul! / My uncle!" (1.5.40-1), help to explain his behavior toward Claudius in act 1, scene 2? (What had Hamlet's soul prophesied?)

9. The Ghost personifies virtue and lust (1.5.53-7):

a. What will virtue never do?

b. What will lust do?

c. What does the Ghost imply about his "most seeming-virtuous queen" (1.5.46)?

d. How would you feel if you were hearing a ghost in the figure of your dead father say this about your mother?

10. Look carefully at the imagery the Ghost uses to describe the effects of the poison—"the cursed hebenon"—on his body (1.5.60-73). What figurative language does the Ghost use to describe his body? List two or three key phrases. Then choose some part of the description and sketch it:

11. Consider the imagery of the king's body, and consider again the beginning of the Ghost's narration of his murder that includes, "So the whole ear of Denmark . . ." (1.5.35-40). Given the Ghost's story of how he died, what does the Ghost's figurative language imply about the relationship between king and state?

12. The Ghost tells Hamlet that he was "Cut off even in the blossoms of my sin, / Unhouseled, disappointed, unaneled" (1.5.76-7). (*Unhouseled* means "not having had the Eucharist administered" [OED]; *disappointed* can mean "not adequately appointed or prepared" [OED 2]; *unaneled* means "not having received extreme unction" [OED].) What was King Hamlet not able to do before he died? How does this help explain why his ghost would be doomed to walk the night?

13. "If thou has nature in thee, bear it not" (1.5.81). What does the Ghost specify that a natural son should not bear? What does the Ghost imply would be a son's response to his father's murder? What, then, does the Ghost imply would be the reason Prince Hamlet would not avenge the murder of King Hamlet?

14. "But howsoever thou pursuest this act, / Taint not thy mind, nor let thy soul contrive / Against thy mother aught" (1.5.84-6). If Hamlet pursues the act the Ghost has demanded, do you think he also will be able to follow these further instructions? How or how not?

15. What is the Ghost's final command (1.5.91)? Quote it:

16. If you were performing Hamlet, what clues would the "Os" in his response to the Ghost give you about Hamlet's state of mind (1.5.92-3)?

17. Reread Hamlet's response upon the Ghost's exit (1.5.95-112):

    > Remember thee?
    > Ay, thou poor ghost, whiles memory holds a seat
    > In this distracted globe. Remember thee?
    > Yea, from the table of my memory
    > I'll wipe away all trivial fond records,
    > All saws of books, all forms, all pressures past,
    > That youth and observation copied there,
    > And thy commandment all alone shall live
    > Within the book and volume of my brain,
    > Unmixed with baser matter. [. . .]
    >   Now to my word.
    > It is "Adieu, adieu, remember me."
    > I have sworn't.

    a. How many times does Hamlet say *remember* and *memory*?

    b. To what might Hamlet refer by "this distracted globe"? Give two possible readings of, "Ay . . . while memory holds a seat / In this distracted globe" (1.5.96-7), derived from two different meanings of the word *globe*:

    c. Considering that the theater of Shakespeare's company was called The Globe, what additional meanings might the phrase "while memory holds a seat / In this distracted globe" suggest?

    d. Analyze Hamlet's extended metaphor, "Yea, from the table of my memory . . . Unmixed with baser matter" (1.5.98-104):

    <u>vehicle</u>   :   <u>tenor</u>

e. If you were directing *Hamlet*, what might you have Hamlet do as he says, "My tables—meet it is I set it down / That one may smile, and smile, and be a villain" (1.5.107-8)? Would you call for a prop? Give two possible stage directions. (*Tables* here means *writing tablets* or *slate*.)

f. What exactly has Hamlet sworn (1.5.110-12)?

18. What does Hamlet tell Horatio and Marcellus about his conversation with the Ghost? What does he withhold? What does he ask them to swear?

19. After the Ghost exhorts Horatio and Marcellus to "Swear by [Hamlet's] sword," with what tone might Hamlet say, "Well said, old mole!" (1.5.161-2)? Why do you suppose Hamlet's calling the Ghost a "mole" has made scholars suspect that when *Hamlet* first was performed at The Globe, the Ghost exited through a trap door on the floor of the stage?

20. Hamlet: "As I perchance hereafter shall think meet / To put an antic disposition on" (1.5.171-2). (*Meet* here means "suitable" or "fit" (*OED* 2); *antic* means "grotesquely amusing or playful; absurd, fantastical" [*OED* adj. 1]). What does Hamlet go on to explain they might see him do? Quote a relevant phrase or two. What does Hamlet ask them to swear?

21. Imagine you are playing Hamlet. What might motivate you to consider putting on an antic disposition? Give two possibilities.

22. "The time is out of joint. O cursèd spite, / That ever I was born to set it right" (1.5.188-9). What might make Hamlet feel the "time" is "out of joint"? Why the *time*?

23. Review the scene. List (with citations) what the Ghost has demanded that Hamlet do. List what Hamlet has said or sworn he will do.

ACT 2, SCENE 1

1. What does Polonius instruct Reynaldo to do in France? How does he want him to accomplish this task?

2. Look through Polonius and Reynaldo's exchange (2.1.1-73), and read Reynaldo's responses aloud. What do Reynaldo's responses tell you about how Reynaldo—Polonius's servant—feels about Polonius's instructions?

3. What new do we learn about Polonius from what and how he speaks to Reynaldo? Quote three lines or phrases and explain what they show.

4. "You laying these slight sullies on my son, / As 'twere a thing a little soiled i'the working" (2.1.39-40): To what does Polonius compare his son, Laertes? How does his view of his son Laertes compare to his view of his daughter Ophelia?

5. Polonius sums up his instructions with a metaphor: "Your bait of falsehood takes this carp of truth" (2.1.63).

   a. Analyze the metaphor.

vehicle	:	tenor
bait		
carp		

   b. Draw a quick sketch of it.

   c. What does Polonius's metaphor imply about learning the truth? Think about the metaphor's fishing vehicle. To what extent does the metaphor support his theory of how Reynaldo can learn the truth about Laertes? To what extent does it complicate the theory?

6. Act out what Ophelia describes that Hamlet has done (2.1.75-100). If possible, find a partner and each take a role.

   a. How does Polonius understand Hamlet's behavior?

   b. Given what we have heard of Hamlet's plans, what else could account for his behavior?

   c. Imagine performing the role of Ophelia. How would your Ophelia understand Hamlet's visit? Why would your Ophelia tell your father about the visit?

7. Reread:

   > I am sorry that with better heed and judgment
   > I had not quoted him. I feared he did but trifle,
   > And meant to wrack thee—but beshrew my jealousy!
   > (2.1.111-13)

   quoted=observe; trifle=treat without respect
   wrack=ruin; beshrew=curse ; jealousy=suspicion

   a. Compare what Polonius now says about Hamlet to what he had told Ophelia earlier about giving Hamlet "private time" (1.3.90-135). How has Polonius's view of Hamlet's attention to Ophelia changed?

   b. What do Polonius's new view of Hamlet and his admitted mistake in judgment move him to do?

   c. EXTRA OPPORTUNITY. How else might a father have reacted? Imagine what else Polonius might have said, starting with 2.1.117.

   Come, _____

   _____

   _____

   _____

ACT 2, SCENE 2

1. What "need" does Claudius explain is the cause of his "hasty sending" for Rosencrantz and Guildenstern (2.2.1-18)?

2. How is Claudius's plan for Rosencrantz and Guildenstern similar to Polonius's for Reynaldo? How is it different?

3. What does Gertrude promise Rosencrantz and Guildenstern that their "visitation shall receive" (2.2.21-6)?

4. What do Rosencrantz and Guildenstern say about their Majesties' request?

5. What does Gertrude say when Claudius tells her that Polonius has found the cause of Hamlet's "distemper" (2.2.54-7)?

    a. Quote her lines.

b. Keeping in mind that Gertrude and Claudius are alone on stage at this point, what do we learn about Gertrude's view of her marriage and her son's condition? What do we learn about her relationship with Claudius?

6. From where have the ambassadors, Voltemand and Cornelius, returned?

7. What does Voltimand report about the King of Norway and his nephew, Fortinbras?

8. Explain Norway's "entreaty" for Fortinbras's "quiet pass / Through [Denmark's] dominions" (2.2.76-8).

9. Consider Claudius's handling of the conflict with Norway. Reread 1.1.80-107 (starting, "Our last king") and 1.2.17-39 (starting, "Now follows that you know young Fortinbras"). What is Claudius's approach to foreign conflict? How does it compare to what we know of King Hamlet's approach to foreign relations?

10. Given the way Polonius speaks to Claudius and Gertrude, what do you think of his declarations, "I will be brief" (2.2.92) and "I use no art at all" (2.2.95)? Derive your answer from specific context.

11. Why, according to Polonius, has Ophelia given him her letter from Hamlet?

12. What might motivate Polonius to read the letter to the King and Queen? Give two possibilities.

13. What reason, in his letter, does Hamlet give for being "ill at these numbers" (2.2.119)? (*Numbers* means *verses*.) Consider the poem Polonius reads: do you think Hamlet is "ill" at numbers?

14. What does the King's question, "But how hath she /Received his love" (2.2.27-8), indicate about Claudius's attitude toward Hamlet and Ophelia's relationship? How does Claudius's attitude compare to that of Polonius and Laertes?

15. When Claudius asks Gertrude what she thinks of Polonius's theory of Hamlet's madness, Gertrude says, "It may be, very like" (2.2.151). How can you account for the discrepancy between Gertrude's comment here and her earlier comment about Hamlet's "distemper," namely: "I doubt it is no other but the main, / His father's death, and our o'erhasty marriage" (2.2.55-7)? Give two possibilities.

16. What might motivate Ophelia to turn her love letter over to her father? Consider the effect her action has and her possible motivations. Indicate two effects and two possible motivations.

17. What does Polonius propose so that they may "try" his theory of Hamlet's madness further (2.2.158)?

18. Reread:

    Hamlet For if the sun breed maggots in a dead dog, being a good kissing carrion—Have you a daughter?
    Polonius I have, my lord.
    Hamlet Let her not walk i'th' sun. Conception is a blessing: but as your daughter may conceive, friend, look to't. (2.2.180-4)

    a. Consider Hamlet's use of the word *sun* and try to explain how he connects the breeding of maggots to the possibility that Ophelia may conceive. What meanings of *sun* might Hamlet be hinting in "Let her not walk i'th' sun"? Give two possibilities.

    b. *To conceive* can mean to become pregnant—to receive seed in the womb— (*OED* 1), and it can mean to understand—to admit an idea into the mind (*OED* 6, 9). Explain the possible pun in Hamlet's warning Polonius that his "daughter may *conceive*." (*For an explanation of* pun, *see question 8 on page 11.*)

19. Reread:

    Pol. What do you read, my lord?
    Ham. Words, words, words.
    Pol. What is the matter, my lord?
    Ham. Between who?
    Pol. I mean the matter that you read, my lord.   (2.2.189-93)

    If Hamlet is trying to persuade Polonius that he is antic or mad, what does his speech imply he believes to be the nature of a mad person's language? Derive your answer from the exchange above.

20. As Polonius leaves and Rosencrantz and Guildenstern enter, Hamlet remarks, "These tedious old fools" (2.2.215). In the Second Quarto and the First Folio, the stage direction, "Enter Guildenstern and Rosencrantz," follows Hamlet's remark. *(For explanations of* Second Quarto *and* First Folio, *see appendix 3, "On How an Edition of* Hamlet *is Made," on pages 104-6.)* If Hamlet refers to the departing Polonius, what does the remark indicate about Hamlet's behavior during their recent conversation?

21. How does Hamlet greet Rosencrantz and Guildenstern?

22. EXTRA OPPORTUNITY. After some (often bawdy) banter, Hamlet eventually charges, "You were sent for" (2.2.274-5). If you were directing the play, at what point would you have your Hamlet suspect his friends? Choose a specific line and explain how it would provoke or how it expresses suspicion.

23. When Guildenstern admits that they were sent for (2.2.288), Hamlet tells them why and describes his condition: "I have of late . . . lost my mirth . . . congregation of vapors" (2.2.291-8).

    a. How does Hamlet's description of his behavior and world outlook compare to what we know of how Hamlet was feeling and behaving before he encountered the Ghost? Quote something that Hamlet has said or that another character has said about him.

    b. What since the encounter with the Ghost might further account for the behavior and world outlook Hamlet describes?

24. Note that Rosencrantz tells Hamlet that a company of "players" is on its way to court "to offer [him] service" (2.2.309-12). Reread:

Hamlet	Gentlemen, you are welcome to Elsinore. Your hands, come then: th' appurtenance of welcome is fashion and ceremony. Let me comply with you in this garb, lest my extent to the players, which, I tell you must show fairly outwards, should more appear like entertainment than yours. You are welcome.—But my uncle-father and aunt-mother are deceived.
Guildenstern	In what, my dear lord?
Hamlet	I am but mad north-north-west. When the wind is southerly I know a hawk from a handsaw. (2.2.360-70)

a. Underline Hamlet's terms related to clothing and acting.

b. What kind of welcome, finally, does Hamlet announce that he is extending to his friends? In what "garb" is he complying?

c. How does Hamlet compare his welcome of Rosencrantz and Guildenstern to his upcoming welcome of the players?

d. What is the effect of Hamlet's referring to Claudius and Gertrude as "uncle-father" and "aunt-mother"?

e. How, according to Hamlet, are they "deceived"? What does Hamlet likely mean when he says he is "but mad north-north-west"? And what do his references to wind directions imply about his alleged madness?

f. If you were Rosencrantz or Guildenstern, what would you think about Hamlet's condition after your exchange with him? How would you feel about having been sent for by the king and assigned the task of "glean[ing] / Whether aught to [Claudius] unknown afflicts" Hamlet (2.2.16-17)? What choices would you have?

25. EXTRA RESEARCH OPPORTUNITY. What did Jephthah do? (Consult the biblical Book of Judges.) What does Hamlet imply about Polonius when he calls him "Jephthah" (2.2.393)?

26. After welcoming the players, Hamlet asks for a speech. What does he emphasize about the speech he requests (2.2.421-31). What does he mean when he says that the speech was "caviare to the general" (2.2.423-4)?

27. Hamlet asks the player to perform "Aeneas' tale to Dido [. . .] especially where he speaks of Priam's slaughter" (2.2.432-4). (Pyrrhus, the son of Achilles, was summoned to the Trojan War to avenge his father Achilles, who was killed by Priam's son Paris. Virgil's *Aeneid* tells the story of how Pyrrhus murdered Priam while Priam was praying at the altar—and while Priam's wife, Hecuba, was watching.) Hamlet begins to recite the speech at 2.2.436 ("The rugged Pyrrhus, like th' Hyrcanian beast"); the First Player recites from 2.2.456-504 ("Anon he finds him" . . . And passion in the gods.")

   a. How is the avenger Pyrrhus described in this speech? Quote two or three key phrases.

   b. When Pyrrhus first strikes at Priam, he "strikes wide" and misses, but the "unnervèd" Priam falls down (2.2.458-60). What is the consequence of Pyrrhus's attempted strike? What happens to "senseless Ilium" when its king, though alive and uninjured, falls down? (*Ilium* is another name for Troy.)

   c. After Pyrrhus strikes again and kills Priam, the speech details Queen Hecuba's reaction. What, according to the speech, would anyone "Who this had seen" do (2.2.496)?

d. How does this account of the effect of King Priam's death in Ilium compare to what we've heard about King Hamlet's death in Denmark? How is Hamlet's situation like Pyrrhus's? How is if different?

e. Look again at how Hamlet begins the speech he wants the player to recite:

"The rugged Pyrrhus, like th'Hyrcanian beast"—
'Tis not so—It begins with Pyrrhus—
"The rugged Pyrrhus, he whose sable arms. . . (2.2.436-8)

What is different about the second way Hamlet begins the speech? What simile describing Pyrrhus does he excise? With what does he replace it? Possible significance?

28. When Hamlet requests a performance of "The Murder of Gonzago," what else does he request of the First Player?

29. Read Hamlet's "rogue and peasant slave" soliloquy aloud (2.2.532-92). Then work through the following questions:

a. Using what Hamlet goes on to describe, explain what he refers to when he says that "this player . . . / Could force his soul so to his own conceit" (2.2.534-6).

b. Why does Hamlet find it "monstrous" that the player could do so (2.2.534)? Cite specific clues in the speech.

c. What does Hamlet imagine the player would do if he had the "motive and the cue for passion" (2.2.544) that Hamlet has?

d. In what context is the word *cue* primarily used? What, then, does the word *cue* indicate about how Hamlet now imagines his own situation?

e. What might Hamlet mean when he says that he "can say nothing" (2.2.553)? Why might he feel this way?

f. Hamlet concludes that he must be "pigeon-livered and lack gall" (2.2.562) or he already would have "fatted all the region kites / With this slave's offal" (2.2.564-5). (A *kite* is a bird of prey [*OED* 1]; an *offal* is the body or limbs of a slaughtered animal or slain person [*OED* 2b].) Who is "this slave"? What does Hamlet imagine he already would have done were he not a coward?

g. Hamlet says that he has been "prompted to [his] revenge by heaven and hell" (2.2.570). In what way might Hamlet think that he has been prompted to his revenge by heaven? In what way by hell? What are the implications for Hamlet's revenge plan? What are the implications for Hamlet's soul?

h. EXTRA OPPORTUNITY. Hamlet thinks that "unpack[ing]" his "heart with words" makes him "like a whore" (2.2.571). How might this be so? How does this complaint about the kinds of words he is speaking compare to his previous complaint that he "can say nothing"?

i. For what purpose does Hamlet plan to "have these players / Play something like the murder of [his] father" (2.2.581-2)?

j. What has Hamlet "heard" about "guilty creatures" at plays that justifies his plan (2.2.576-9)?

k. Consider: "I'll observe his looks, / I'll tent him to the quick. If he but blench, / I know my course" (2.2.583-5). How exactly does Hamlet plan to determine whether or not Claudius is one of these guilty creatures he has heard about? What do you think of his plan?

l. "The spirit that I have seen / May be a devil, and the devil hath power / T'assume a pleasing shape" (2.2.585-7). What is Hamlet's worry about the Ghost? Where have we heard this idea before?

m. Hamlet says, "I'll have grounds / More relative than this" (2.2.590-1). (*Relative* means, "Having application or reference *to*" or "Having relation to the question or matter in hand; pertinent, relevant" [*OED* 4a & b].) In what way might Hamlet think that his plan to "catch the conscience of the King" will give him grounds more "relative" for killing Claudius than what he has heard from a ghost (2.2.592)?

n. What do you think of Hamlet's proposed method of figuring out whether the Ghost was the spirit of his father or a devil in a pleasing shape? If you were in Hamlet's situation, what would you do if you were unsure?

o. "The play's the thing / Wherein I'll catch the conscience of the king" (2.2.591-2). Any similarities to other characters' plans and statements? List them.

p. EXTRA OPPORTUNITY. Read the soliloquy through once more as if preparing to perform it. What do you notice about the way it is structured? What clues are there for shifts in tone? Which words would you give special emphasis? Where and how does it change subject? What do its rhythms and structure reveal about the way Hamlet is feeling and thinking?

ACT 3, SCENE 1

1. What do Rosencrantz and Guildenstern report to the king and queen? What do they not report? How would you assess their response to being asked by the King to spy on Hamlet?

2. When Claudius hears that Hamlet has requested the performance of a play, he directs Rosencrantz and Guildenstern, "Good gentlemen, give him a further edge, / And drive his purpose into these delights" (3.1.26-7). Consider what we know of Hamlet's purpose, and explain the dramatic irony of this direction.

3. What might motivate Claudius to ask Gertrude to leave him and Polonius to be "lawful espials" of Hamlet and Ophelia (3.1.32)?

4. How does Gertrude respond to Claudius's request? What does she tell Ophelia before she leaves?

5. After instructing Ophelia to "Read on this book"—likely a prayer book—to "color" her being alone, Polonius adds, "We are oft to blame in this: / 'Tis too much proved that with devotion's visage / And pious action we do sugar o'er / The devil himself" (3.1.44-9).

    a. To what does the *this* in "blame in *this*" refer?

    b. What, according to Polonius, can sugar over the devil himself?

c. Polonius implies, wittingly or not, that he is instructing his daughter to cover over something devilish. What will Ophelia be covering while pretending that she is reading or praying?

d. Considering his own assessment of what he asks Ophelia to do, what might motivate Polonius to continue, nonetheless, the plan of "loos[ing]" his daughter to Hamlet (2.2.161)?

6. Claudius agrees with Polonius that shows of devotion and pious actions can sugar over the devil. Analyze his analogy:

> O, 'tis too true!
> How smart a lash that speech doth give my conscience!
> The harlot's cheek, beautied with plastering art,   *harlot=prostitute; plastering art=make-up*
> Is not more ugly to the thing that helps it
> Than is my deed to my most painted word.
> O heavy burden!   (3.1.49-54)

harlot's cheek   :

beautied   :

plastering art   :

a. What is Claudius's painted word? What is his deed?

b. Why his *painted* word? What would be an *unpainted* word?

c. To what "heavy burden" does Claudius refer?

d. What do we learn about Claudius from his acknowledgment here?

7. Reread "To be, or not to be" (3.1.56-88) aloud; then answer the following questions from Hamlet's point of view.

   a. What variation do you notice in the iambic pentameter of Hamlet's first lines? Effect? *(See page 96 of appendix 1, "Listening for Meter.")*

   b. Hamlet begins with the question "To be, or not to be." What second question follows this one? Are the two questions related? How or how not?

   c. What in Hamlet's first two questions might lead him to think death—"To die" (3.1.60)?

   d. What is appealing about death? How is death a "consummation / Devoutly to be wished" (3.1.63-4)?

   e. How is "perchance to dream" the "rub" to the appeal of death (3.1.65)?

   f. What is the "quietus" that one could make with a "bare bodkin" (3.1.75-6)?

   g. What would people not have to bear if they would make their quietus with a bare bodkin? How does Hamlet describe life (3.1.76-7)?

h. What stops people from doing so?

i. With what metaphor does Hamlet describe death (3.1.79)? Quote it.

j. What is ironic about Hamlet's saying that "no traveller returns" from death (3.1.80)?

k. How does "conscience [. . .] make cowards of us all" (3.1.83)? What does conscience keep us from doing?

l. What "hue" (*color*) would be "native" (*natural*) to "resolution"? What does the "pale cast of thought" do to it (3.1.84-5)?

m. EXTRA OPPORTUNITY. Hamlet uses the image of a falcon at "great pitch" to illustrate how an enterprise loses "the name of action" (3.1.86-8). Explain the comparison.

n. By the end of the speech, to what extent—if any—has Hamlet answered his initial question, "To be, or not to be"? How so?

8. Upon seeing Ophelia, Hamlet says, "Nymph, in thy orisons / Be all my sins remembered" (3.1.88-9). (*Orisons* means *prayers*.) If you were playing Hamlet, how would you perform these lines? Does he speak to himself? To Ophelia? With what tone? Write a stage direction for him.

9. If Ophelia is "reading" a prayer book as her father instructed, does she fool Hamlet? Explain.

10. Reread the exchange between Hamlet and Ophelia (3.1.88-148).

    a. What might be motivating Ophelia in this scene? Why do you think she has agreed to be a part of this testing of Hamlet arranged by her father and the king? List at least two possibilities.

    b. What about Hamlet? How might he feel seeing Ophelia? What might motivate the way he behaves toward her? List at least two possibilities.

    c. What does Ophelia wish to "re-deliver" to Hamlet (3.1.94)? How does Hamlet respond?

    d. What does Hamlet mean when he tells Ophelia, "We are arrant knaves, all: believe none of us" (3.1.128)? (*Arrant* means "notorious" [*OED* 3]; a *knave* is a "dishonest, unprincipled man" [*OED* 3a].) Who is "we"? How does Hamlet's assertion support his insistence that Ophelia go to a nunnery?

e. Reread lines 136-148 ("Or, if thou wilt needs marry . . . To a nunnery, go"). Of what, specifically, does Hamlet accuse Ophelia and women in general? How, for example, can women make "monsters" of men? And what infuriates Hamlet's about women's make-up?

f. Review Ophelia's responses to Hamlet throughout the scene. Read Ophelia's lines aloud—without reading Hamlet's lines. What is the tone of her responses to Hamlet at first? At what point do her responses change in tone? What does Hamlet ask and what does Ophelia respond just before this change?

g. To what extent, if any, is Hamlet's anger at Ophelia justified? Give your reasons.

h. After Hamlet exits, Ophelia proclaims, "O, what a noble mind is here o'erthrown!" (3.1.149). Considering the circumstances and outcome of her meeting with Hamlet, give two or three possibilities of what Ophelia might be thinking and feeling at this point.

i. EXTRA OPPORTUNITY. In Shakespeare's day, *honest* could mean "chaste" (*OED* 3b) and *nunnery* could mean "brothel" (*OED* 1b). Do you think Hamlet uses both senses of these words? In which lines? If so, do you think Ophelia understands his punning?

j. EXTRA OPPORTUNITY. Some critics and directors imagine that Hamlet has overheard the conversation between Polonius and Claudius and is thus speaking to Ophelia knowing that he will be overheard. Do you agree? Refer specifically to the text as you explain why or why not.

11. What is Claudius's assessment of Hamlet's behavior? What does Claudius decide to do?

12. What is Polonius's response? What new plan does he suggest to the king?

ACT 3, SCENE 2

1. Reread Hamlet's instructions to the players, which begins, "Speak the speech, I pray you" and concludes, "Go, make you ready" (3.2.1-41). (*Player* is another word for actor, *playing* for acting.)

   a. What does Hamlet promote as the correct method of acting?

   b. The "groundlings" (3.2.10) were play audience members with the least expensive tickets: they stood on the ground in front of the stage. What kind of playing does Hamlet assert appeals to them? What is Hamlet's attitude toward them?

   c. What does Hamlet say is "the purpose of playing" (3.2.19)? Quote the phrase.

   d. Consider the style of Hamlet's speech here. Does it recall anyone else's speech? Whose?

   e. If you were the First Player, how would you feel about hearing all of these instructions from your patron, the Prince? How would you deliver your responses to Hamlet (3.2.14; 3.2.33-4)?

   f. What is Hamlet's worry about the effect of the clowns on the play's audience (3.2.35-40)?

   g. Given Hamlet's purpose in arranging the play, why might he be particularly eager to control the clowns?

2. When Horatio arrives, Hamlet praises him abundantly (3.2.50-70). What advantage, according to Hamlet, comes from Horatio's "blood and judgment" being "so well commeddled" (3.2.64-7)? (*Blood* means passion [*OED* 12]; *judgment* means discretion, wisdom [OED 1b].) Quote key words and phrases in your answer.

3. Hamlet asks Horatio to join him in observing Claudius at the play: Hamlet now imagines that his and Horatio's "judgments" will "join / In censure of [Claudius's] seeming" (3.2.82-3). What does Hamlet's request suggest about Hamlet's attitude toward his plan to catch the conscience of the king? Do you think including Horatio in his plan is a good idea?

4. As Claudius, Polonius, Gertrude, Ophelia, and others arrive for the play, Hamlet says, "I must be idle" (3.2.86). How does he go on to behave? If you were an unsuspecting courtier who had come to see the play, what would you think of Hamlet's behavior?

5. EXTRA OPPORTUNITY. Reread Hamlet's interaction with Claudius (3.2.88-92).

   Claudius   How fares our cousin Hamlet?
   Hamlet   Excellent, i'faith, of the chameleon's dish. I eat the air, promise-crammed.

   Claudius rejects Hamlet's mistaking of his use of the word *fares* to mean "eats" instead of his intended "does": "I have nothing with this answer, Hamlet. These words are not mine" (3.2.88-92). Hamlet quips, "No, nor mine now" (3.2.93). What does Hamlet's quip point out about the nature of words?

6. In the Yale edition, the stage direction that follows Hamlet's question, "Lady, shall I lie in your lap?" (3.2.106), reads "HE LIES AT OPHELIA'S FEET," a stage direction not in any early text of *Hamlet* but first introduced by editor Nicholas Rowe in 1709.

   a. What does Hamlet's question suggest about where he is proposing to lie?

   b. What stage direction would you write if you were editing the play?

   c. Especially given the public nature of the event, how would you feel if you were Ophelia? In what tone of voice might Ophelia say "No, my lord" (3.2.107)? What might you be trying to communicate to Hamlet? Give two possibilities.

7. Hamlet persists in his bawdy remarks. How do Hamlet's quips about "country matters" and "nothing" as "a fair thought to lie between maids' legs" recall his earlier concern about conception (3.2.110-4)? (In Shakespeare's day, *thing* could mean *penis*, and *nothing* could mean *vagina*.) Look carefully at how Ophelia responds and think about ways to perform her lines.

8. A "dumb show" (a play with gestures but no words) precedes the performance of "The Murder of Gonzago."

   a. What is enacted in this particular dumb show? Stage directions for it, which are printed in the Second Quarto and the First Folio, directly follow 3.2.128. *(For explanations of* Second Quarto *and* First Folio, *see appendix 3, "On How an Edition of* Hamlet *is Made," on pages 104-6.)*

   b. What do you suppose might have motivated directors who have staged this scene with Claudius distracted and not watching the dumb show?

   c. If Claudius sees the dumb show—and there's no indication in any text that he doesn't—what questions does the dumb show raise about Hamlet's plan to "catch the conscience of the king"? List three.

d. What might Ophelia be thinking about the dumb show? With what tone might she ask, "What means this, my lord" (3.2.129)? Give two possibilities.

9. Reread the dialogue between the Player King and the Player Queen (3.2.144-219). What echoes of the situation in Elsinore do you hear? What echoes of the Ghost's story? List three.

10. What do Hamlet's comments during the play reveal about his concerns and motivations? Quote one or two and explain what you think each reveals.

11. "This is one Lucianus, nephew to the King" (3.2.234).

    a. Hamlet says that the "purpose of playing" is to hold "the mirror up to nature." If by staging *The Murder of Gonzago* Hamlet is trying to mirror what the Ghost told him about King Hamlet's death, how, in fact, would Lucianus be related to the Player King?

    b. If Hamlet mistakenly identifies Lucianus as "nephew," what are the consequences for Hamlet's plan to catch the conscience of King Claudius?

    c. If Hamlet purposefully identifies Lucianus as "nephew," what might motivate him to do so? How would this motivation affect his plan to catch the king's conscience?

d. How might members of the audience who do not suspect King Claudius of any wrong doing interpret Hamlet's identifying Lucianus as the nephew and the King's abrupt departure? In other words, what more ordinary tension might a courtier imagine would exist between Prince Hamlet and his uncle who recently was elected king while the prince was away at school?

12. Think of three ways Claudius might demand, "Give me some light. Away!" (3.2.258), indicating three different reactions to the play and Hamlet's behavior and comments. Write three different stage directions.

13. How does Hamlet interpret the king's departure?

14. Note carefully what Horatio says—and what he doesn't say—in response to Hamlet's questions, "Didst perceive?" (3.2.275) and "Upon the talk of poisoning?" (3.2.277). How does Horatio respond? What might he be thinking? Give two or three possibilities.

15. What do Rosencrantz and Guildenstern tell Hamlet about Claudius and Gertrude? How does Hamlet respond?

16. What does Hamlet mean when he asks Rosencrantz and Guildenstern, "do you think I am easier to be played on than a pipe" (3.2.352-53)? Has Hamlet attempted to "play upon" (3.2.354) anyone?

17. Reread Hamlet's speech that concludes the scene (3.2.371-82). It begins "'Tis now the very witching time of night."

    a. How is Hamlet feeling at what he calls "the witching time of night" (3.2.371)?

    b. Hamlet warns himself, "O heart, lose not thy nature. Let not ever / The soul of Nero enter this firm bosom. / Let me be cruel, no unnatural" (3.2.376-8)? Nero was an emperor of Rome who murdered his mother. What does Hamlet imply is unnatural for a son?

    c. What do these instructions to his own heart reveal that Hamlet feels like doing?

    d. Remember that the Ghost told Hamlet, "If thou has nature in thee, bear it not" (1.5.81). What did the Ghost imply was natural for a son?

    e. What do you think of Hamlet's decision to "speak daggers to her, but use none" (3.2.379)?

    f. How does Hamlet imagine that his "tongue and soul" will "be hypocrites" (3.2.380)?

ACT 3, SCENE 3

1. In response to Claudius's assertion that he is sending Hamlet to England because he is not "safe" with Hamlet near (3.3.1), Rosencrantz speaks a simile and then an extended metaphor to describe the "cess" (cessation, stoppage) of kingship.

   a. Underline the simile; put parentheses around the extended metaphor.

   > The cess of majesty
   > Dies not alone; but, like a gulf doth draw
   > What's near it with it. It is a massy wheel,
   > Fixed on the summit of the highest mount,
   > To whose huge spokes ten thousand lesser things
   > Are mortised and adjoined, which when it falls,
   > Each small annexment (petty consequence!)
   > Attends the boist'rous ruin. (3.3.15-22)

   b. Then, indicate the main vehicle of each figure.

vehicle	:	tenor
_____	:	cess of majesty
	or	
_____	:	it

   c. Choose either the simile or the metaphor and sketch it:

   d. How would Rosencrantz's view of kingship apply to the current state of Denmark? Does the view of kingship affect your opinion of Hamlet's plan to murder Claudius? How or how not?

2. What does Polonius plan to do while Hamlet visits Gertrude in her closet? (*Closet* here means a *private room*.) Why, according to Polonius, should there be "some more audience than a mother" (3.3.31)?

3. Reread Claudius's soliloquy that begins, "O, my offence is rank" (3.3.36-72): it is one of the few instances we hear from Claudius when he's not speaking publically.

   a. How does Claudius describe his "offence" (3.3.36)?

   b. Why can't Claudius pray even though his "inclination" is "as sharp as will" (3.3.39)?

   c. Claudius asks of his "cursèd hand": "Is there not rain enough in the sweet heavens / To wash it white as snow" (3.3.43-6). Claudius answers his own question by asking another question about the purpose of mercy: "Whereto serves mercy / But to confront the visage of offense?" (3.3.46-7). What is Claudius reviewing about the nature of God's mercy? What does Claudius know about his ability to receive mercy, to be forgiven?

   d. Claudius reminds himself that the purpose of prayer is "two-fold"— either "forestall[ing]" a sin or being "pardoned" having sinned (3.3.48-50). If Claudius knows that prayer can lead to forgiveness for a sin committed, why does he think that there is not an adequate prayer for his situation? Quote what Claudius says that best explains his reasoning:

e. What does Claudius point out is different about justice in "this world" (3.3.57) and "above" (3.3.60)?

f. Considering what Claudius has asked about being pardoned and retaining the offence (3.3.56), what might be going through Claudius's mind when he encourages himself to try to pray?

g. Having studied this soliloquy, what do you think of Claudius now?

4. Why exactly does Hamlet decide not to kill Claudius while "he is praying" (3.3.73-96)?

5. How is Hamlet's decision ironic given the couplet that ends Claudius's attempt at prayer, "My words fly up, my thoughts remain below: / Words without thoughts never to heaven go" (3.3.97-8)?

6. How does Hamlet's misinterpretation of Claudius while he is attempting to pray affect your understanding of Hamlet's method of trying to "catch the conscience of the king"?

ACT 3, SCENE 4

1. Reread the exchange below without stage directions, as they were printed in the early texts:

Hamlet	Come, come, and sit you down, you shall not budge.
	You go not till I set you up a glass
	Where you may see the inmost part of you.
Gertrude	What wilt thou do? thou wilt not murder me? Help, ho!
Polonius	What, ho! Help, help, help! (3.4.18-22)

   What action is implied in this exchange? Write a stage direction each for Hamlet, Gertrude, and Polonius. Indicate what each character is doing.

2. What does Hamlet's question, "Is it the king?" (3.4.26), indicate about his stabbing through the arras? What does Hamlet say once he sees that it is Polonius whom he has killed? What do you think of Hamlet's reaction?

3. Read aloud Gertrude's responses to Hamlet's murdering Polonius and to what Hamlet says to her (3.4.25, 29, 38-9, 51-2). What do you think these responses indicate about Gertrude's knowledge of her former husband's death?

4. After Hamlet shows Gertrude images of her former husband, the late King Hamlet, and her current husband, King Claudius, he asks her, "Have you eyes? / Could you on this fair mountain leave to feed / And batten on this moor" (3.4.65-7). Analyze the metaphor Hamlet uses for marriage. (*Batten* can mean "to feed *esp.* of animals" or "to feed gluttonously on" (*OED* 1a, 1b); *moor* means "a marsh or marshland" or "a piece of unenclosed waste ground" [*OED* 1, 2].)

vehicle	:	tenor
feed	:	
fair mountain	:	
batten	:	
moor	:	

5. Hamlet then asserts:

   You cannot call it love; for at your age
   The hey-day in the blood is tame, it's humble
   And waits upon the judgment, and what judgment
   Would step from this to this? (3.4.68-71)

   What does Hamlet say could *not* have motivated Gertrude "at [her] age" to marry Claudius? How does this assertion compare with his previous metaphor? How does it compare to other assertions Hamlet and the Ghost have made about Gertrude? Be specific.

6. What reason does Gertrude give when she asks Hamlet to "speak no more" (3.4.88)?

7. Note well: "O, speak to me no more. / These words like daggers enter in my ears" (3.4.94-5). Why do you think Hamlet keeps talking despite his mother's plea?

8. What is the effect of the Ghost's entrance? Why would Gertrude conclude, "Alas, he's mad" (3.4.105)?

9. Reread:

    > Do not look upon me,
    > Lest with this piteous action you convert
    > My stern effects. Then what I have to do
    > Will want true color—tears perchance for blood. (3.4.127-30)

    a. To what does Hamlet refer when he says, "what I have to do"?

    b. What does Hamlet imply is the "true color" of what he has to do? (Hint: what is the color of blood?)

    c. Why does Hamlet not want pity? How does he fear it would affect him?

    d. How does Hamlet's understanding of revenge and pity compare to the Ghost's (1.5.5)?

    e. Many editors include a stage direction indicating that Hamlet addresses these words to the Ghost. To whom else might they be addressed?

10. Why does Gertrude think the Ghost is "the very coinage of [Hamlet's] brain" (3.4.137)?

11. Analyze the metaphor in Hamlet's instruction to Gertrude:

    Lay not that flattering unction to your soul,
    That not your trespass, but my madness speaks.
    It will but skin and film in the ulcerous place,
    Whiles rank corruption, mining all within,
    Infects unseen. Confess yourself to heaven,   (3.4.145-9)

    <u>vehicle</u>   :   <u>tenor</u>

    _____   :   flattering

    unction   :   _____

    skin and film   :   _____

    ulcerous place   :   _____

    rank corruption   :   _____

    mining all within,
    infects unseen   :   _____

    _____   :   confess yourself to heaven

    What does this image of the effect of a covered, infected wound on the body imply about an undisclosed, unconfessed "trespass" or sin on the soul?

12. Reread Hamlet's instruction after he tells Gertrude, "go not to mine uncle's bed"—starting from "Assume a virtue, if you have it not . . . (3.4.160). Read through line 170 ("With wondrous potency"), and then answer the following:

   a. What "virtue" is Hamlet telling his mother to "assume"?

   b. Explain Hamlet's assertion that "use almost can change the stamp of nature" (3.4.168). What is *use*? What is *the stamp of nature*?

   c. What "nature" does Hamlet imagine Gertrude has that "almost" can be changed by "use"? What "use" would change it?

   d. How does what Hamlet says here about virtue compare to the Ghost's assertion that virtue "never will be moved" (1.5.53-4)?

   e. How does it compare to Laertes's claim that "Virtue itself 'scapes not calumnious strokes" (1.3.38)?

   f. What do you think about these various theories of virtue? What is your theory of virtue?

g. EXTRA OPPORTUNITY. Hamlet personifies custom as a monster who eats all sense.

> That monster, custom, who all sense doth eat,
> Of habits devil, is angel yet in this,
> That to the use of actions fair and good
> He likewise gives a frock or livery,
> That aptly is put on.   (3.4.161-5)

Think about what a *custom* is and what *sense* is, and then explain why the monster custom would eat all sense. (It might help to think about what motivates someone to do something out of *custom*.)

How does Hamlet's speech invoke two meanings of *habit*? (*Habit* can mean "dress or attire characteristic of a particular rank, degree, profession, or function; *esp.* the dress of a religious order" (*OED* 2) or a "tendency to act in a certain way, *esp.* one acquired by frequent repetition of the same act until it becomes almost or quite involuntary . . . a custom" [*OED* 9].)

In what way, according to Hamlet, can custom also be an angel?

How does this idea of custom further explain Hamlet's advice that Gertrude should "Assume a virtue"?

13. What does Hamlet bid his mother do (3.4.181-8)? What does Hamlet's use of the double negative ("Not this, by no means, that I bid you do") prompt him to describe in detail?

14. If you were Gertrude, what would you think of your son Hamlet's parting remarks about Polonius, starting with "I'll lug the guts into the neighbor room" (3.4.212-16)? What would you think about Hamlet's condition now? What would you think about your marriage? What would you feel you could or should do about the situation?

ACT 4, SCENE 1

1. What does Gertrude report to Claudius?

2. Given Gertrude's promise that she will not "breathe" what Hamlet has said to her (3.4.198), how do you interpret Gertrude's report? What seems to be her motivation? Give two possibilities.

3. What does Claudius say when he hears of Polonius's murder?

4. EXTRA OPPORTUNITY. Analyze Claudius's extended simile comparing "our love . . . like the owner of a foul disease" (4.1.19-23):

   <u>vehicle</u> : <u>tenor</u>

5. When Gertrude tells Claudius that Hamlet has gone "To draw apart the body he hath killed," she describes his madness and tells Claudius that Hamlet "weeps for what is done" (4.1.24-7). Has Hamlet, as far as we know, wept for having killed Polonius? Imagine you are preparing to perform as Gertrude. What would be your motivation for reporting this?

6. What does Claudius mean when he says "[T]his vile deed / We must with all our majesty and skill, / Both countenance and excuse" (4.1.31-2). Why might Claudius tell Gertrude he must both "countenance and excuse" Polonius's murder? (*Countenance* can mean "sanction . . . bear out [*OED* 5].)

ACT 4, SCENE 2

1. Read through the entire short scene. Then reread Hamlet's first line. What is "safely stowed" (4.2.1)? Write a stage direction for Hamlet that would help the audience understand what Hamlet has done just before the scene begins.

2. Explain what Hamlet says to Rosencrantz and Guildenstern about sponges and apes (4.2.15-20).

3. Do you think Hamlet is right about the King's treatment of Rosencrantz and Guildenstern?

4. Reread:

   Hamlet   The body is with the King, but the King is not with the body. The King is a thing—
   Guildenstern A thing, my lord!
   Hamlet   Of nothing. Bring me to him. (4.3.26-9)

   List everything to which "body" could refer in the lines above:

   List everything or everyone to which "King" could refer:

   If you were performing the role of Hamlet, what would you have Hamlet mean? Which body? Which king? Fill in the blanks:

   The body [of _____] is with the King [_____], but the King [_____] is not

   with the body [of _____]. The King [_____] is a thing—

ACT 4, SCENE 3

1. What reasons does Claudius give for not putting "the strong law" on Hamlet (4.3.3)?

2. How does Hamlet go on to explain his quip that Polonius is "At supper" (4.3.17)?

3. How does Hamlet explain how "a king may go a progress through the guts of a beggar" (4.3.30-1)?

4. If you were preparing to perform Hamlet, what would you imagine is motivating your character's treatment of Polonius's body and macabre jokes about it?

5. How does Hamlet explain calling Claudius "mother" (4.3.48)?

6. After Rosencrantz and Guildenstern exit, what do we learn that Claudius has arranged, by letter, for Hamlet's arrival in England?

ACT 4, SCENE 4

1. Reread Fortinbras's opening speech. Fortinbras orders the Captain to tell "the Danish king" that he "[c]raves the conveyance of a promised march / Over his kingdom" (4.4.1-4). Where are Fortinbras and his army headed? When and for what purpose might this march (over Denmark) have been promised? (Hint: Review Claudius's dispatch of Cornelius and Voltemand in act 1, scene 2.)

2. When speaking to Hamlet, how does the Norwegian Captain describe the land for which they will fight (4.4.17-22)?

3. Analyze the metaphor in Hamlet's concluding remark: "This is th'impostume of much wealth and peace, / That inward breaks, and shows no cause without / Why the man dies" (4.4.27-9). (An *impostume* is an abscess [*OED* 1] or infected lesion.)

    What does this metaphor imply about how Hamlet judges the pending battle for this land?

4. Reread Hamlet's soliloquy aloud that begins, "How all occasions do inform against me" (4.4.32-66). Then read it again, and answer the following questions.

   a. How would the "occasion" of Fortinbras's march "inform against" Hamlet and "spur [his] dull revenge" (4.4.32-3)?

   b. According to Hamlet, what activities make a man "A beast, no more" (4.4.35)?

   c. Hamlet asserts, "Sure he that made us with such large discourse, / Looking before and after, gave us not / That capability and god-like reason / To fust in us unused" " (4.4.36-9)? What does Hamlet imply about how he is behaving by not taking revenge?

   d. Hamlet then imagines his inaction possibly caused by something other than "Bestial oblivion" : explain what he says about "thinking too precisely on th'event" and the "quartered" thought (4.4.41-3). When have we heard Hamlet think this before?

   e. How exactly does Hamlet describe Fortinbras and his military project? What is the "eggshell" for which Fortinbras fights (4.4.53)?

   f. What does Hamlet say about being great? About honor (4.4.53-6)?

g. How does Hamlet compare his situation to that of Fortinbras's army (4.4.56-65)?

h. What does Hamlet say motivates the soldiers to "go to their graves like beds" Quote the phrase:

   "That for a _____ and _____ of _____" (4.4.61).

i. What conclusion does Hamlet draw from his argument? What does he exclaim?

j. What other conclusion could be drawn from Hamlet's argument? Explain how.

ACT 4, SCENE 5

1. Why do you think Gertrude refuses to speak to Ophelia (4.5.1)? Give two possibilities.

2. What does the Gentleman report about Ophelia? What is she doing? About what is she speaking?

3. Reread the Gentleman's remark:

   > Her speech is nothing,
   > Yet the unshaped use of it doth move
   > The hearers to collection. They aim at it,
   > And botch the words up fit to their own thoughts, (4.5.7-10)

   What does the Gentleman mean by "nothing"? What kind of hearing are the "hearers" doing?

4. With what reasoning does Horatio convince Gertrude to see Ophelia?

5. Right before Ophelia enters, what does Gertrude, who is briefly alone, say about guilt (4.5.17-20)?

6. Consider Ophelia's first songs, starting, "How should I your true love know" (4.5.23); "He is dead and gone, lady" (4.5.29); and "Larded with sweet flowers" (4.5.38). About what does she sing?

7. EXTRA OPPORTUNITY. Listen to the meter and scan these lines of Ophelia's song. *(See appendix 1, pages 93-6, "Listening for Meter.")* Although some editors omit the "not" of line 39, the word is printed in all three of the early *Hamlet* texts.

    White his shroud as the mountain snow

        Larded with sweet flowers

    Which bewept to the grave did not go

        With true-love showers.   (4.5.36-40)

    What do the irregularities in the song's meter call attention to?

8. How does Gertrude respond to Ophelia? How does Claudius respond to her?

9. Does Claudius's assessment, "Conceit upon her father" (4.5.45), seem right? Why or why not?

10. Consider Ophelia's next song, starting "To-morrow is Saint Valentine's day" and continuing "By Gis and by Saint Charity" (4.5.48-66).

    a. What happens to the "maid" who the young man lets in the chamber door?

    b. How does the young man respond to her complaint, "before you tumbled me, / You promised me to wed" (4.5.63-4)?

c. If Ophelia has gone mad or is "distract" (4.5.2), as the Gentleman says, then what do her behavior and these songs suggest about what has distracted or is troubling her?

11. Note Claudius's assessment of Ophelia's condition after Ophelia leaves, starting "O, this is the poison of deep grief" (4.5.75).

   a. What does Claudius imply "deep grief" can do?

   b. What does Claudius admit about Polonius's burial when he says "we have done but greenly / In hugger-mugger to inter him" (4.5.83-4)? (*Hugger-mugger* means *secretly*.)

   c. If Claudius has buried Polonius hugger-mugger, then what has Ophelia not had the opportunity to do? What might she not know? How does her situation compare to Hamlet's?

   d. Claudius describes "Poor Ophelia," as "Divided from herself and her fair judgment, / Without the which we are pictures, or mere beasts" (4.5.84-6). In what way would someone without judgment be like a picture? In what way like a beast?

12. With what imagery does Claudius describe what Laertes has been hearing upon his return (4.5.87-94)? Quote key phrases.

13. Look for clues for staging Laertes's entrance and confrontation of Claudius. Quote a few key phrases:

14. Explain the logic of Laertes's response to Gertrude's suggestion that he remain calm:

    > That drop of blood that's calm proclaims me bastard,
    > Cries cuckold to my father, brands the harlot
    > Even here, between the chaste and unsmirchèd brow
    > Of my true mother. (4.5.116-20)

    What would Laertes have to believe in order to feel that if one drop of his blood were calm, he would be named a bastard, his father a cuckold, and his mother a harlot?

    How does Laertes's belief about revenge compare to the Ghost's?

15. Claudius says, "Let him go, Gertrude. Do not fear our person. / There's such divinity doth hedge a king / That treason can by peep to what it would / Acts little of his will" (4.5.122-5).

    a. What must Laertes be doing? What must Gertrude be doing? Write a stage direction for each or sketch the moment.

    b. How does Claudius reassure Gertrude that she should not "fear" his "person"? How is his explanation ironic?

16. How does Claudius handle Laertes in his rage? Is his method effective?

17. Of what does Ophelia sing when she enters now?

18. EXTRA OPPORTUNITY. To whom do you think Ophelia gives which flowers (4.5.174-83)? (None of the early texts includes stage directions here.) In many productions, Ophelia hands out objects other than flowers. If you were directing *Hamlet*, what would you have her hand out?

19. About what does Laertes express concern: "His means of death, his obscure funeral [. . .] That I must call't in question" (4.5.210-14)?

ACT 4, SCENE 6

What do we learn from Hamlet's letter to Horatio? List the key points.

ACT 4, SCENE 7

1. Notice, throughout this scene, how Claudius manages Laertes. What explanation does Claudius give for his not having punished Hamlet for the murder of Polonius?

2. Why do you think Hamlet, having escaped his execution, would send a letter to Claudius about his return to Elsinore?

3. What previous event makes Laertes's stated willingness to "cut [Hamlet's] throat i'the church" (4.7.124) especially poignant?

4. What do Laertes and Claudius plan?

5. Read carefully Gertrude's description of Ophelia's death, starting, "There is a willow grows askant the brook" (4.7.165-82). With what images does Gertrude describe Ophelia and the circumstances of her drowning?

ACT 5, SCENE 1

Read the clown-gravedigger scene aloud with a friend and try to notice how the jokes and wordplay work. Imagine you are preparing to direct the play: try to decide if the gravediggers are joking intentionally or if they remain unaware of the humor of their speech.

1. What question does the gravedigger ask about Ophelia's burial (5.1.1-2)? How would it matter if "she drowned herself in her own defense" (5.1.5-6)?

2. What privilege, according to the gravedigger, comes from Ophelia's having been a "gentlewoman" (5.1.22)? What's funny about the gravedigger's observation, "And the more pity that great folk should have countenance in this world to drown or hang themselves, more than their even-Christen" (5.1.24-6)?

3. In the back-and-forth about Adam (starting at "There is no ancient gentlemen but gard'ners"), how does the joke on *gentlemen* and *arms* work (5.1.27-35)? Who else have you seen perform this kind of wordplay?

4. What does Horatio say when Hamlet wonders that the gravedigger can sing while grave-making (5.1.61-3)? Quote Horatio's line and note what previous line(s) his comment echoes.

5. How does Hamlet feel about the gravedigger's handling of the skulls? What does the sight of the bones make Hamlet imagine?

6. Reread:

   > *Hamlet*   Whose grave's this, sirrah?
   > *Clown 1* Mine, sir. . . .
   > *Hamlet*   I think it be thine, indeed, for thou liest in't.
   > *Clown 1* You lie out on't, sir, and therefore it is not yours. For my part, I do not lie in 't, and yet it is mine. . . .
   > *Hamlet*   What man dost thou dig it for?
   > *Clown 1* For no man, sir.
   > *Hamlet*   What woman, then?
   > *Clown 1* For none, neither.
   > *Hamlet*   Who is to be buried in't?
   > *Clown 1* One that was a woman, sir; but rest her soul, she's dead. (5.1.109-24)

   Hamlet's concludes about the gravedigger: "How absolute the knave is" (5.1.125). What do you think he means by "absolute"? Do you agree with Hamlet's conclusion?

   Compare this exchange to the one between Hamlet and Polonius in act 2, scene 2. Similarities? Differences?

7. When Hamlet asks the gravedigger why Hamlet was sent to England, the gravedigger replies, "Why, because 'a was mad. 'A shall recover his wits there, or, if 'a do not, it's no great matter there" (5.1.138-9). Explain the joke made at an English audience's expense.

8. Follow what the gravedigger says about how long he has been a grave-maker. How old is Hamlet?

9. Do you think the gravedigger would know that the skull he gives Hamlet is Yorick's? Why or why not? Do you think Hamlet believes the gravedigger knows that it is Yorick's skull? How would you direct the actors in this scene?

10. What concern does Hamlet express when he asks Horatio if he thinks Alexander (the Great) "looked o'this fashion i'th'earth" (5.1.182-3)?

11. What are "maimèd rites" (5.1.203)? In what way and for what reason are Ophelia's rites maimèd? What other burial rites have been maimèd?

12. What does Gertrude do and say at Ophelia's grave (5.1.228-30)? How do Gertrude's remarks (starting at "I hoped thou shoudst") affect your understanding of Polonius and Laertes's assessment of Ophelia's relationship with Hamlet?

13. Note that "the Dane" is another way of saying the King of Denmark. (Marcellus, for instance, declares his loyalty to the king by announcing that he is "liegemen to the Dane" [1.1.15].) What does Hamlet claim when he declares, "This is I, Hamlet the Dane" (5.1.242-3)? What seems to provoke Hamlet to make this claim at this moment?

14. What else does Hamlet do and say at Ophelia's grave? Does any of it clarify how he feels about Ophelia? What do you think provokes his actions?

15. What must Hamlet not to be thinking about when he asks Laertes, "What is the reason that you use me thus" (5.1.274)?

ACT 5, SCENE 2

1. Consider what Hamlet tells Horatio about finding Claudius's commission ordering his execution, and then explain why Hamlet praises "rashness" and asserts that "There's a divinity that shapes our ends" (5.2.7, 10). How does Hamlet understand his escape?

2. With what did Hamlet replace King Claudius's commission? What did Hamlet have with him that enabled him to do so?

3. What does Horatio mean when he asks, "So Guildenstern and Rosencrantz go to't" (5.2.56)? Consider Hamlet's response, "Why, man, they did make love to this employment" (5.2.57), and then write a stage direction for how Horatio should deliver his line.

4. What offenses does Hamlet list now before asking "is't not perfect conscience / To quit him with this arm" (5.2.67-8)? How do the reasons Hamlet gives for killing Claudius here differ from reasons he has expressed before? Be specific.

5. EXTRA OPPORTUNITY. How does Hamlet make fun of Osric? Do you think Osric's behavior warrants Hamlet's mocking? Why or why not?

6. Carefully reread the brief conversation between Hamlet and Horatio, starting with Horatio's warning, "You will lose this wager, my lord" (5.2.195-209).

   a. With what explanation does Hamlet dismiss his observation, "how ill all's here about my heart" (5.2.198)? How does he characterize his feeling?

   b. What does Horatio advise?

   c. What does Hamlet suggest with his allusion to the Gospel According to Matthew, "There's a special providence in the fall of a sparrow" (5.2.205-6)? (*Providence* means "The foreknowing and protective care of God . . . ; divine direction, control, or guidance [*OED* 2].)

   d. What leads Hamlet to say, "Let be" (5.2.209)?

   e. Do you think Hamlet has answered the question, "To be, or not to be" (3.1.56)? If so, how?

7. Summarize Hamlet's request for Laertes's pardon (5.2.211-29). If you were Laertes, how would you feel about Hamlet's apology?

8. Hamlet says he'll be Laertes's "foil" (5.2.240). Considering that Hamlet then explains, "In mine ignorance / Your skill shall, like a star i'the darkest night, /Stick fiery off indeed" (5.2.240-2), Hamlet's use of the word *foil* suggests the definition, "A thin leaf of some metal placed under a precious stone to increase its brilliancy" (*OED* 5). Do you agree that Hamlet is Laertes's *foil* in this sense? With specific reference to Hamlet's imagery, explain how or how not.

9. What else can the word *foil* mean? How else is the word used in this scene? Give two (or more) additional definitions and explain how each meaning expands the idea of Hamlet as Laertes's foil.

10. Explain how Gertrude, Laertes, and Hamlet each is poisoned.

11. What exactly does Hamlet say before he stabs Claudius with the envenomed sword? Quote the two lines:

12. What do Hamlet's question and assertion suggest is the immediate motivation for his murder of Claudius?

13. Note the exchange between Laertes and Hamlet after Laertes asks Hamlet to "exchange forgiveness" with him:

    Laertes Mine and my father's death come not upon thee,
             Nor thine on me.
    Hamlet   Heaven make thee free of it.   (5.2.316-18).

    What kind of exchange of forgiveness occurs? What do you think of Laertes's and Hamlet's pleas that their souls be free of these murders? Why might they think it possible?

14. Hamlet says, "Had I but time . . . O, I could tell you" (5.2.322-4). What would Hamlet tell? What do you think Hamlet wants Horatio to report?

15. "I am more an antique Roman than a Dane. / Here's yet some liquor left" (5.2.327-8). What does Horatio want to do? How does Hamlet convince Horatio not to do this?

16. What follows Hamlet's last words, "The rest is silence," and Horatio's farewell (5.2.344-7)?

17. What does Fortinbras mean when he says that he has "some rights of memory in this kingdom" (5.2.375)?

18. What type of funeral does Fortinbras plan for Hamlet? Do you think it is fitting?

APPENDIX 1. LISTENING FOR METER—AN INTRODUCTION

Actors have long observed that Shakespeare's plays convey their meanings not only through the sense of his language but also through its sounds, including rhyme, alliteration (repeated consonant sounds), and assonance (repeated vowel sounds). Read aloud and consider how the sounds of a speech contribute to its meanings.

This section will help you get started listening for the rhythms of a Shakespeare play by introducing you to the meters, and their variations, that you will encounter in *Hamlet*.

> ❧ For most English literature, **METER** refers to a deliberate pattern of stressed and unstressed syllables.
>
> *"Stressed" syllables are the syllables that get the most emphasis when a word or sentence is spoken aloud. (In the literature of some other languages, including Greek and Latin, meter is measured by the length rather than the stress of syllables.)*
>
> *Keep in mind that you can hear the meter in which a poet has composed a speech or poem even while you can hear how the poet has, at times, varied that meter.*
>
> ❧ In a Shakespeare play, speeches in **VERSE** are composed with a repeating pattern of stressed and unstressed syllables and are divided into deliberate lines. Verse is composed in meter.
>
> ❧ In a Shakespeare play, speeches in **PROSE** are composed without a repeating pattern of stressed and unstressed syllables and are not divided into deliberate lines. Prose is not composed in meter.

Examples of VERSE in *Hamlet*:

> *Ophelia*   He took me by the wrist and held me hard;
>   Then goes he to the length of all his arm
>   And, with his other hand thus o'er his brow,
>   He falls to such perusal of my face
>   As 'a would draw it.   (2.1.87-91)

> *Hamlet*
>   The time is out of joint. O cursèd spite,
>   That ever I was born to set it right!   (1.5.188-9)

> ❧   The lines of Hamlet's speech above, which have the same meter and end with a rhyme, are called a **COUPLET**.

- When you are reading verse, you will see that the first word of each new line of a speech is capitalized whether or not it begins a new sentence.

- Whatever the size of a book's pages, printers retain the lines of a speech in verse. Thus, often you will see empty space between the end of a line and the right margin of your book's page. If a line of verse is longer than what fits on a particular page, then what remains of the verse line usually is indented and printed directly below.

- When you quote verse, you should retain the capital letters and indicate the line breaks with a forward slash, called a *virgule*. Example: Hamlet decides that "The play's the thing / Wherein [he]'ll catch the conscience of the king" (2.2.591-2).

An example of PROSE in *Hamlet*:

> *Hamlet*   Speak the speech, I pray you, as I pronounced it to you,
>   trippingly on the tongue. But if you mouth it as many of
>   your players do, I had as lief the town-crier spoke my lines. (3.2.1-3)

- When you are reading prose, you will see that lines are printed until a word nearly reaches the right margin of the page. The first word of a new line, which varies depending on the size of the book, is not capitalized unless it happens to begin a new sentence.

🙢 An **IAMB** is a poetic foot of one unstressed syllable (marked "˘") followed by one stressed syllable (marked "/"). Examples of single words that are iambs are:

$$\breve{u}\acute{p}on \qquad \breve{r}e\acute{v}enge$$

˘ /
upon

˘ /
revenge

🙢 **IAMBIC PENTAMETER** names the meter of a line of verse with five ("penta") iambs. An example:

˘ / ˘ / ˘ / ˘ / ˘ /
It faded on the crowing of the cock. (1.1.157)

🙢 Marking the stressed and unstressed syllables of a line of verse in the manner above is called **SCANSION**. To **SCAN** a line of verse is to listen for and mark its stressed and unstressed syllables and to notice what kind and how many of the repeating foot make up the line. Scansion also includes noticing any variations in the meter of a line. *(See page 96 for examples of variations in iambic pentameter).*

🙠 **BALLAD METER** names the metrical structure of a four-line stanza that alternates between **IAMBIC TETRAMETER** (a line of verse with four ("tetra") iambs) and **IAMBIC TRIMETER** (a line of verse with three ("tri") iambs) and whose second and fourth lines rhyme. An example:

⏑ / ⏑ / ⏑ / ⏑ /
By Gis and by Saint Charity,
⏑ / ⏑ / ⏑ /
Alack, and fie for shame!
⏑ / ⏑ / ⏑ / ⏑ /
Young men will do't, if they come to't.
⏑ / ⏑ / ⏑ /
By Cock, they are to blame.   (4.5.58-61)

Note that the contractions of "do it" as "do't" and "to it" as "to't" become one stressed syllable each and keep the meter of the line.

🙠 A **TROCHEE** is a poetic foot of one stressed syllable followed by one unstressed syllable. Examples of single words that are trochees are:

/ ⏑   / ⏑
nothing   murder

🙠 **TROCHAIC TETRAMETER** names the meter of a line with four ("tetra") trochees. **TROCHAIC TRIMETER** names the meter of a line with three ("tri") trochees. The verses of one of Ophelia's songs alternate between trochaic tetrameter and trochaic trimeter:

/ ⏑ / ⏑ / ⏑ /
How should I your true love know
/ ⏑ / ⏑ /
From another one?
/ ⏑ / ⏑ / ⏑ /
By his cockle hat and staff,
/ ⏑ / ⏑ /
And his sandal shoon.

🙠 *You will notice that these lines lack the unstressed syllable of their final trochee. Thus, the first and third lines are called* **CATALECTIC TROCHAIC TETRAMETER**; *the second and fourth lines are called* **CATALECTIC TROCHAIC TRIMETER**.

Much of *Hamlet* is composed in iambic pentameter, but you will hear many variations in the meter. Below are two to listen for. Consider what a variation calls attention to and what it may add to a speech's meanings.

> Some iambic lines replace one of the iambs with a trochee, a **TROCHEE SUBSTITUTION**. Here's an example of an iambic pentameter line that begins with a trochee substitution:

$$/\ \smile\ \smile\ /\ \smile\ /\ \smile\ /\ \smile\ /$$
Murder most foul, as in the best it is,   (1.5.27)

And here's an example of a midline trochee substitution:

$$\smile\ /\ \smile\ /\ /\ \smile\ \smile\ /\ \smile\ /$$
To give them seals—never, my soul, consent!   (3.2.382)

> Some iambic lines end with an extra unstressed syllable. Such a line is said to have a **FEMININE ENDING**. An example:

$$\smile\ /\ \smile\ /\ \smile\ /\ \smile\ /\ \smile\ /\ \smile$$
To be, or not to be: that is the question.   (3.1.56)

Note that an alternate reading of the above line would include a midline trochee substitution:
$$\smile\ /\ \smile\ /\ \smile\ /\ /\ \smile\ \smile\ /\ \smile$$
To be, or not to be: that is the question.

Sometimes a line of verse is spoken by more than one character. Here is a single iambic pentameter line shared by Claudius and Gertrude:

Claudius   Our son shall win.

Gertrude   He's fat, and scant of breath.   (5.2.273)

And here is a single iambic pentameter line shared by Laertes, Claudius, and Gertrude:

Laertes   Where is my father?

Claudius   Dead.

Gertrude   But not by him.   (4.5.128)

Note that the above line begins with a trochee substitution.

APPENDIX 2. READING FIGURATIVE LANGUAGE—
AN INTRODUCTION TO METAPHOR, SIMILE, METONYMY, & SYNECDOCHE

Shakespeare's plays are famous for their figures of speech, which are rich in meaning and sometimes difficult to understand. What follows is an introduction to four key figures of speech—metaphor, simile, metonymy, and synecdoche—along with some techniques you can use as you work to understand them.

> ✒ A **METAPHOR** asserts that one thing is another thing and demands that we imagine how it can be so.
>
> "A rose is a flower" is not a metaphor. A rose is **LITERALLY** a flower. Anyone could find this out by looking up "rose" in a dictionary.
>
> "Love is a rose" is a metaphor because it demands that we imagine how love is like a rose. A metaphor can be understood as true only if taken **FIGURATIVELY**.

Our English word *metaphor* is borrowed from Greek. "*Meta*" means *trans-* or *across*, and "*phor*" means *port* or *carry*; thus, *metaphor* can be translated as *transport*. The metaphor above transports a *rose* from the world of gardening to explain something in the world of emotions, namely, *love*. Metaphors explain something in one world by transporting something from a distant world for comparison.

One way to analyze a metaphor is to sort its TENOR and VEHICLE, terms coined by I. A. Richards in his 1936 book *The Philosophy of Rhetoric*.

> ✒ The **TENOR** is the subject of the metaphor—what the speaker is talking about.
>
> ✒ The **VEHICLE** is what is transported for comparison to illuminate some quality of the tenor.
>
> In the metaphor "love is a rose," *love* is the tenor and *rose* is the vehicle.

The combination of a metaphor's vehicle and tenor prompts you to recognize that you're hearing or reading a metaphor because the statement would be otherwise absurd or impossible. As Richards emphasizes, the interaction of the tenor and the vehicle produces the metaphor's meaning.

Take, for example, the opening of Shakespeare's Sonnet 68:

> Thus is his cheek the map of days outworn,

When we read this line, we realize that a literal cheek cannot also be a literal map, and so we know that we're reading a metaphor. Here *cheek* is the tenor—what the speaker is talking about—and *map* is the vehicle—what the speaker has transported from the world of diagrams, paper, and ink to describe "cheek" by comparison.

Sometimes it is helpful to sort the metaphor's vehicle and tenor in a chart:

vehicle	:	tenor
map	:	cheek

And sometimes it is helpful to sketch the metaphor, trying to show both its vehicle (cheek) and its tenor (map). Here is an example:

G. Minette

> ❧ A **SIMILE** asserts that one thing is "like" or "as" another thing and demands that we imagine how.

"Lucinda is like her grandmother" is not a simile. It is a **LITERAL** statement.

"Lucinda is like a hurricane" is a simile. It is a **FIGURATIVE** statement.

Of course we may have to figure out how Lucinda is like her grandmother, but comparing Lucinda and her grandmother—who both are human, female, and kin—doesn't demand that we use our imagination to find similarities in altogether different categories of things as we must if we are to understand how a human being is like a storm.

Like metaphors, similes work by comparison, but with the word *like* or *as*, similes indicate their comparisons more explicitly. Similes announce the relationship between the tenor and vehicle more formally. When Rosencrantz describes the consequences of the death of a king, he speaks a simile:

> The cess of majesty
> Dies not alone; but, like a gulf doth draw
> What's near it with it.   (3.3.15-17)

Here Rosencrantz transports a *gulf*—a whirlpool—to describe what happens in a country when its king dies—*the cess of majesty*. (*Cess* means *cessation* or *stoppage*.) You could chart the simile:

vehicle	:	tenor
gulf	:	cess of majesty

The metaphor that opens Sonnet 68 articulates both tenor and vehicle—the cheek and the map—and makes clear their relationship: the cheek "is" the map. Sometimes, however, a metaphor does not name both tenor and vehicle. Or sometimes a metaphor does not state so clearly how the vehicle corresponds to the tenor. Such metaphors require more interpretation. Consider, for example, Hamlet's plan for his visit to his mother:

>I will speak daggers to her, but use none.   (3.2.379)

We know that Hamlet speaks a metaphor because he cannot be planning literally to speak *daggers* to his mother. But Hamlet doesn't say explicitly what he plans to speak that corresponds to "daggers," so we need to interpret.

We can start interpreting the metaphor by charting:

vehicle	:	tenor
daggers	:	?

Then, we can make a logical interpretation based on the context of Hamlet's statement. Sometimes that context suggests more than one interpretation. For instance, we could say:

vehicle	:	tenor
daggers	:	cruel, hateful words *(that will make Gertrude feel hurt by her son's cruelty)*

Or we could say:

vehicle	:	tenor
daggers	:	truthful words *(that will make Gertrude feel hurt once aware of her guilt)*

Sometimes a statement or speech articulates more than one part of a metaphor's vehicle or tenor. Take, for example, Barnardo's comment as he tries to persuade Horatio to believe that he and Marcellus have twice seen a ghost:

> *Barnardo* Sit down awhile;
> And let us once again assail your ears,
> That are so fortified against our story
> What we have two nights seen.   (1.1.30-3)

Here are four steps that can help lead to an accurate and productive analysis of such a metaphor. I have included sample analysis for each step.

STEP 1. IDENTIFY THE METAPHOR'S SPEAKER, AUDIENCE, & CONTEXT.

Jot down speaker and audience, and briefly review the immediate and relevant context of the speech.

Example:

> Barnardo to Horatio. Horatio has joined Barnardo and Marcellus on the watch but does not believe that they have seen a ghost the previous two nights.

STEP 2. IDENTIFY THE METAPHOR'S VEHICLES.

Underline all the elements of the metaphor's vehicle in the speech.

> *You can find a metaphor's vehicle by looking for the parts that would be absurd if taken literally with the tenor. Here, for instance, you can recognize that "fortified" is part of the vehicle because it would be absurd to imagine that Barnardo is saying that Hamlet's ear literally has a fort built up around it.*

Example:

> *Barnardo* Sit down awhile;
> And let us once again <u>assail</u> your ears,
> That are so <u>fortified</u> against our story
> What we have two nights seen.

STEP 3. SORT THE METAPHOR'S VEHICLE & TENOR.

    A. Start by listing the elements of the vehicle and tenor the speaker states explicitly. Leave blank spaces for the corresponding parts of the vehicle and tenor implied.

Example:

vehicle	:	tenor
assail	:	?
?	:	ears*
fortified against	:	?
?	:	story

The word ears here is itself a figure of speech—a metonymy for Horatio's hearing and believing. (See page 103 for an explanation of metonymy.)

    B. Then, think about the analogies and fill in those blanks.

You might find it helpful to identify the worlds of the vehicle and the tenor. For instance, the vehicle here is from the world of battle and the tenor from the world of speaking and listening.

As you think about the analogies, be sure to review the full list of meanings of any key words. (To analyze this metaphor, you will need to know that assail *means* assault.*)*

As you identify missing parts of the vehicle, you might find it helpful to ask yourself questions like: "With what would someone literally assail something?" Or: "What would be literally fortified?"

As you try to understand the tenor, you might find it helpful to ask yourself questions like: "How could an ear be like something fortified?" Or: "What could be done to an ear that would be like assailing a fortified structure?"

Remember that filling in the blanks requires interpretation and that there may be more than one way to interpret accurately.

Example:

vehicle (world of battle)	:	tenor (world of speaking and listening)
assail	:	speak into
castle or citadel or city	:	ears
fortified against	:	disbelieving of
weapon	:	story

102

STEP 4. ARTICULATE THE METAPHOR'S MEANINGS & IMPLICATIONS.

First, think carefully about the metaphor's specific vehicle. In the case of this metaphor, think about the qualities of battles, fortifications, and weapons. Then, think about how the qualities of the vehicle are transported onto the metaphor's tenor.

Keep in mind that not all of the implications and meanings of a metaphor are necessarily intended by the character who speaks the metaphor. Even if a metaphor's implications are not intended by a character, they nonetheless can acquire meaning in the play.

Example:

> Barnardo's metaphor compares Horatio's unwillingness to listen to and believe that Barnardo and Marcellus have seen a ghost to a castle or city that has been prepared to resist an enemy attack. Barnardo's metaphor implies that Horatio has anticipated an attack and has protected—"fortified"—himself against the story of the ghost's existence. The metaphor further implies that Barnardo's speech about the ghost's appearance is somehow like a violent enemy determined to break into the disbelieving Horatio. Horatio's "ears" will be "assailed" by their story, which is figured as the weapon of an intruding enemy. If an enemy successfully assails a fortified city or building, it typically either takes over or steals what is valuable and leaves the rest in ruins. The metaphor suggests that if Barnardo were to succeed in penetrating Horatio's disbelief and persuading him, then Horatio would be violently changed by the story of the ghost. Barnardo's metaphor implies that hearing and accepting something one previously has found to be unbelievable can be a violent and transforming experience.

Whereas metaphor and simile work by comparison, metonymy and synecdoche work by association or scale.

- One thing standing for another associated thing is called **METONYMY**.

Polonius uses metonymy when he advises Laertes, "Give every man thy ear" (1.3.68). An *ear* is associated with listening, so "give . . . thy ear" stands here for listening.

- Part of a thing standing for the whole thing is called **SYNECDOCHE**.

Hamlet uses synecdoche when he says of Polonius's dead body, "I'll lug the guts into the neighbor room" (3.4.212). *Guts* are part of a body, and the word *guts* stands here for Polonius's entire dead body.

The difference between *being associated with* and *being part of* can be very slim, so it can be difficult to decide whether to classify a figure of speech as metonymy or synecdoche. The difference between metonymy and metaphor, however, is larger and more significant. In order to understand a metaphor or simile we need to imagine how a tenor in one world compares to a vehicle from a distant world: we need to imagine how one thing *is* or *is like* another thing with which it ordinarily is not associated. Unlike metaphor and simile, metonymy and synecdoche are from the same world as the things they stand for.

APPENDIX 3. ON HOW AN EDITION OF *HAMLET* IS MADE

Anyone who publishes a Shakespeare play has made a number of decisions about how to transform the earliest surviving copies of the play into a current edition. As you develop your own interpretation of *Hamlet*, it is helpful to be aware of what role an editor has played in making the edition of the play you are reading.

None of Shakespeare's handwritten play manuscripts has survived, and as far as anyone knows, Shakespeare was not involved in the publication of his plays. While Shakespeare was still alive, some of his individual plays were published in small books called *quartos*. One quarto of *Hamlet* was published in 1603 (now called the *First Quarto* or *Q1*) and another in 1604 (now called the *Second Quarto* or *Q2*). After Shakespeare's death, *Hamlet* also was included in a collection of Shakespeare's plays, entitled *Mr. William Shakespeares Comedies, Histories, & Tragedies*, which was published in a large book called a *folio*. (Scholars now refer to this first edition of Shakespeare's collected plays as the *First Folio* or *F1*.)

"To be, or not to be," remains one of the most famous phrases written in English. Almost everyone has heard it, but any editor of the play *Hamlet* must decide how to print it. Here is the beginning of Hamlet's famous soliloquy as it appears in each of the surviving early texts:

The 1603 Quarto

> Cor. And here Ofelia, reade you on this booke,
> And walke aloofe, the King shal be vnseene.
> Ham. To be, or not to be, I there's the point,
> To Die, to sleepe, is that all? I all:

The 1604 Quarto

> Enter Hamlet.
> Pol. I heare him comming, with-draw my Lord.
> Ham. To be, or not to be, that is the question,
> Whether tis nobler in the minde to suffer
> The slings and arrowes of outragious fortune,
> Or to take Armes against a sea of troubles,
> And by opposing, end them, to die to sleepe
> No more, and by a sleepe, to say we end

The 1623 Folio

> *Pol.* I heare him comming, let's withdraw my Lord.
> *Exeunt*
> *Enter Hamlet.*
> *Ham.* To be, or not to be, that is the Queſtion:
> Whether 'tis Nobler in the minde to ſuffer
> The Slings and Arrowes of outragious Fortune,
> Or to take Armes againſt a Sea of troubles,
> And by oppoſing end them: to dye, to ſleepe
> No more; and by a ſleepe, to ſay we end

And here it is as printed in the 2003 Yale University Press edition of the play:

> *Polonius*   I hear him coming. Let's withdraw, my lord.
>   EXEUNT CLAUDIUS AND POLONIUS
>   ENTER HAMLET (THINKING HIMSELF ALONE)
> *Hamlet*   To be, or not to be: that is the question.
>   Whether 'tis nobler in the mind to suffer
>   The slings and arrows of outrageous fortune,
>   Or to take arms against a sea of troubles,
>   And by opposing end them? To die, to sleep
>   No more, and by a sleep to say we end   (3.1.55-60)

The choices editors make about what to include in an edition of *Hamlet* depend on their theories about the sources of the early texts. Some basic information about each:

◦ **The 1603 Quarto.** The *Hamlet* printed in the 1603 Quarto is shorter and, to many readers, not as good as the *Hamlet* of the 1604 Quarto or the First Folio. Some scholars have suggested that this edition of *Hamlet* may have been reconstructed from memory, perhaps that of an actor in the company who had heard the play performed frequently enough to remember much of it, if inaccurately. The 1603 Quarto's title page advertises that it publishes the play, "As it hath beene diurse times acted by his Highnesse seruants in the Cittie of London: as also in the two Vniuersities of Cambridge and Oxford, and elsewhere." (The letters "U" and "V" were interchangeable in Shakespeare's day!)

◦ **The 1604 Quarto.** Many scholars imagine that the play printed in the 1604 Quarto was derived from a manuscript of the play handwritten by Shakespeare. The 1604 Quarto's title page advertises that it is from a more reliable copy than the 1603 Quarto and almost twice as long as it: "Newly imprinted and enlarged to almost as much againe as it was, according to the true and perfect Coppie."

◦ **The 1623 Folio.** Seven years after Shakespeare's death, two of his fellow actors, John Heminges and Henry Condell, collected and edited the thirty-six plays of the First Folio. The First Folio's title page advertises that it contains the plays "Published according to the True Originall Copies."

So, what's an editor to do? None of Shakespeare's handwritten play manuscripts—no "true" or "original" copy—has survived. Moreover, as a playwright who was part-owner of a theater company, Shakespeare very well have may revised his plays during the course of their various performances or adapted them for particular occasions, further complicating the idea of an "original" or "perfect" copy. (*Perfect* can mean *complete*.) Since Shakespeare himself was not involved in the publication of his plays, he did not make any choices about their publication.

There are considerable differences in the three early texts. Here are just a few examples of the variations from which editors must choose:

- Whereas in the 1603 Quarto the King's counselor is named "Corambis," in the 1604 Quarto and 1623 Folio he is named "Polonius."

- In the 1604 Quarto, Hamlet wishes that his "too too *sallied* flesh would melt"; in the 1623 Folio, he wishes that his "too too *solid* flesh would melt" (emphasis mine).

- Neither the 1603 Quarto nor the 1623 Folio includes the soliloquy in the 1604 Quarto that Hamlet speaks upon seeing Fortinbras and the Norwegian army. (The soliloquy, in what is now marked as act 4, begins, "How all occasions do inform against me / And spur my dull revenge!")

- The 1603 Quarto's stage direction for the mad Ophelia's entrance indicates, "*Enter* OFELIA *playing on a lute, and her hair down, singing*," whereas the 1623 Folio indicates "*Enter* OPHELIA *distracted*," and the 1604 Quarto indicates only, "*Enter* OPHELIA."

Many modern editions of *Hamlet* are derived largely from some combination of the 1604 Quarto and the 1623 Folio. However, some recent editors have chosen, instead, to publish a *Hamlet* derived solely from the 1604 Quarto or from the 1623 Folio. Other publishers have printed separate editions of each of the early texts of *Hamlet*. You can compare your edition of *Hamlet* to the early texts by finding facsimiles of them in your library or on the World Wide Web.[1]

You will notice a number of differences between the early quartos and folio and any modern edition of *Hamlet*—regardless of the early text or texts from which the modern edition is derived:

- **Editors standardize spelling and punctuation according to current practices.** So, for instance, the First Folio's "to dye" is printed as "to die."

- **Editors add stage directions not in the Quartos or First Folio.** Often editors distinguish their own stage directions from those in the Quartos or First Folio by enclosing them in parentheses or brackets. So, for instance, the Yale edition prints "Thinking Himself Alone" in parentheses. Editors base such stage directions on their reading of the play, so you should always test them by reading the lines closely and considering other possible stagings. (*See question 9 on page 11 and question 6 on page 57 for exercises on reading an editor's stage directions critically.*)

- **Editors mark act, scene, and line numbers.** The First and Second Quartos do not mark sections of the play with act, scene, or line numbers; the First Folio does not mark line numbers. Editors usually adopt the act and scene numbers marked in the First Folio, to which they add line numbers. Because some speeches in the play are in prose, not verse, a modern edition's line numbers vary depending on the size of the page. (*See pages 93-4 of appendix 1 for explanations of* verse *and* prose.)

- **Editors include notes that explain selected words and phrases.** In some notes editors provide definitions for words that might be unfamiliar to us now or whose meanings were different in Shakespeare's day. For instance, editors often note that the word *sometime* in Claudius's reference to Gertrude as "our sometime sister, now our queen" (1.2.8) means *former*—not *occasional*, as it might now—or that the word *sensible* in "the sensible and true avouch / Of mine own eyes" (1.1.57-8) means *confirmed by one of the senses*. When Claudius refers to "the first corse" (1.2.105), editors usually note that *corse* is an early variant of our word *corpse*. Editors do not list all possible definitions of words they gloss, but you can check the *Oxford English Dictionary* for a complete list of seventeenth-century meanings of any word. In other notes editors may offer more extensive explanations of the meaning of a phrase or a line. Read such notes critically: there may be additional ways to understand the phrase or line.

---

[1] Here are two websites that you might find particularly useful:
The Shakespeare Quarto Archives at http://www.quartos.org/index.html
Internet Shakespeare Editions at http://internetshakespeare.uvic.ca/Library/facsimile/

ACKNOWLEDGMENTS

Over the years I have had the pleasure of reading Shakespeare's *Hamlet* with hundreds of students at Friends Seminary. Their enthusiastic interest in the play, their willingness to work to understand it, and their fresh interpretations have inspired me to develop and publish this guide. I am delighted to have Friends Seminary graduate Laura Simkin Berke's remarkable vision of Elsinore on the cover. I am once again grateful to Robert Lauder, Principal of Friends Seminary, for his gracious support of this project and to my English Department colleagues for their enduring camaraderie and help.

Enabling readers to glimpse the early texts of *Hamlet* is key to helping them understand the sources of the edition they are reading. I am grateful to Michael J. B. Allen for granting me permission to include, on page 104 of this guide, the images of the 1603 and 1604 Quartos scanned from the University of California Press's 1981 facsimile edition, *Shakespeare's Plays in Quarto*, edited by Michael Allen and Kenneth Muir. I am likewise grateful to Donna Anstey at Yale University Press for granting me permission to include, on page 105 of this guide, the image of the First Folio *Hamlet* scanned from the 1954 Yale University Press facsimile edition of *Mr. William Shakespeares Comedies, Histories, & Tragedies*.

The guide's preface and appendices have been shaped by the suggestions of Heather Cross, Chris Doire, Philip Kay, and Sarah Spieldenner, and the text has been improved by Josh Goren's questions and corrections. I am grateful to Patrick Morrissey for our ongoing conversations about meter and figurative language, for his careful reading of the entire manuscript, and for his many suggestions about how to improve the guide's accuracy and clarity. Finally, I am grateful to Gordon Minette for his advice on matters large and small as I prepared *A Guide to Reading Shakespeare's Hamlet* for publication.

www.ingramcontent.com/pod-product-compliance
Lightning Source LLC
Chambersburg PA
CBHW080444110426
42743CB00016B/3273